Lama Ole Nydahl

The Great Seal

LAMA OLE NYDAHL

.

THE GREAT SEAL

LIMITLESS SPACE & JOY

The Mahamudra View of
Diamond Way Buddhism

FIREWHEEL PUBLISHING
SAN FRANCISCO

© 2004 BUDDHISMUS STIFTUNG DIAMANTWEG, Darmstadt
www.buddhismus-siftung.de
ISBN 978-0-9752954-0-3
Library of Congress Control Number: 2004103467

Published by Firewheel Publishing
110 Merced Ave., San Francisco, CA 94127

Distributed to the book trade by Blue Dolphin Publishing, Inc.
P.O. Box 8, Nevada City, CA 95959
Orders: 1-800-643-0765
www.bluedolphinpublishing.com

Printed in the United States of America

5   4   3

Contents

DEDICATION

My interpretations of the wishes of Karmapa are dedicated to the growing number of educated and independent human beings who want to direct their many-sided activities and experiences into a way of enlightenment.

GRATITUDE

Our deepest thanks go to Rangjung Rigpe Dorje, the 16th Karmapa. He transmitted the Great Seal to my wife Hannah and me in Denmark, France, Sikkim, and the United States. Also many thanks to the friends who helped in the making of this book.

FOREWORD

Dear Friends,

This second and more extensive commentary to the *Mahamudra* or Great Seal wishes of the 3rd Karmapa marks the dawning of a new era. Gathering momentum in trains and cars, on flights, and during several short retreats, it was on and off my clipboard over several years. It probably needed to be this way. Surpassing the level of concepts, these verses include every aspect of mind. Enriching the reader's view is much more important than teaching some new terminology. A series of enlightened expressions concerning one's motivation does not easily lend itself to a rigid formulation.

The fluency of this rendition, seven hundred years after it was originally given and in a most different world, brings together my memories of teachings by famous Karma Kagyu lamas, blessings from this lineage, which I shared with my wife Hannah in the Himalayas, and the clear mind of Caty— as well as my own meditations since 1969, blessed by the 16th and the 17th Karmapas. This translation from German in Annett's lovely house in Palm Springs during November 2001 was much improved and anglicized by Stephen of our London Diamond Way Center. While Hannah later provided some traditional points, Anthony and Matt added their common sense. Our North American and Australian centers generously gave up days we should otherwise have shared to make it possible; and a last stay in our center in Graz, Austria, with Axel on his computer, hopefully rounded things off. It is our common aim to pass on Karmapa's ultimate experience of the Great Seal in continually new contexts, while leaving the necessary space for a private understanding. This book should leave you relaxed and confident in the meaning of things and everybody's inherent potential—rather than burdened with additional conceptual baggage.

As the fortress of ignorance should be attacked from all sides, the approach of each verse is different. Every commentary is down to earth and every statement can be directly tested. Contemporary, critical, and even political statements from my side elucidate a timeless text, which points directly to mind's nature. This relevance to the world was the expressed wish of the 16th Karmapa, whose three visits to Europe and North America during the seventies and early eighties—as well as the work of the students he empowered—first opened the West to his view of the Great Seal. These enlightened insights create a sequence of unchanging yet dynamic images, with the first and last verses supplying the necessary conceptual background to absorb Karmapa's experience of the Great Seal. Whoever does not manage to turn into a rainbow after their first reading should be motivated in life by the final verses and make plans for further attempts. For greatest benefit, I recommend reading them not in one sitting but gradually, verse by verse, so that what is understood can settle and one may gain the most out of the timeless values passed on.

The Great Seal wishes transmit the awareness-stream of the Karmapas. After the Karma Kagyu tradition was introduced to the West, these absolute levels of awareness that can be realized through the Great Seal have been the desired goal of an exponentially growing number of Western accomplishers.

Maha translates into "great" and *mudra* means "sign" or "seal" and is derived from a promise that the historical

Author and muse examining some experimental statements from the text.
One hundred meter bungee jump in Axalp, Switzerland.

Buddha gave his closest students 2,500 years ago: "Seek no higher teachings than these, for they do not exist."

My interpretation of the 3rd Karmapa's wishes are dedicated to the growing numbers of educated and independent people who wish to incorporate their multi-faceted lives and experiences into an approach towards enlightenment.

I consciously avoid using the traditional commentaries, in order to keep the book contemporary and its experience fresh. Therefore, the classic outline is placed in an appendix. If any differences are found between my view and an authorized commentary, the latter is of course correct.

Read and enjoy,

Ever Tonh, Laty, Het - Lam Ch.

Yours TCH and Lama Ole

INTRODUCTION

Any observation of the outer and inner worlds refers one to mind. Only mind is constantly and truly present, although not as a substantial "something." Consciousness is like space, unchanging and timeless, while its object, all outer phenomena, as well as the inner states are conditioned; they come and go. Only the experiencer is present always and everywhere.

The Great Seal, *Mahamudra* in Sanskrit or *Chag Chen* in Tibetan, was taught by Buddha in order to fully awaken mind's potential and to seal its enlightened nature. Whoever rests in the radiance of the mirror while enjoying its images and recognizes the indestructibility of the ocean beneath the play of the waves has reached this goal.

The path is a gradually increasing experience of richness and the bliss that enlightenment makes permanent. It begins to manifest in short and less intense forms during the moments when no habits or expectations distract mind. Nonmeditators may also taste some of this power during the free fall before the parachute opens or on a fast motorcycle, and everyone (hopefully) knows it from making love. It appears in a flash when sneezing, as the joyful "a-ha" at a new and striking insight or when one shares the joy or good actions of others. Meditation, however, is the concise and scientific way to make this state permanent. In particular the three "old" or "Red Hat" schools of Tibetan Buddhism, which focus on the Diamond Way practices of view and transformation, can make such moments into a lasting experience. Even a short exchange with a holder of the Great Seal awareness can set off this maturation process, but a close friendship with him or one's co-operation in one of his groups is the most effective method. In meditation and life we will then experience a growing and joyful oneness with phenomena until suffering and frustrations are clearly seen as something unnecessary and odd.

During the 2,500 years since Buddha's death, statements of insight and intent such as: "Space is joy"; "Any event is mind's free play"; "One should see the potential Buddha in all beings"; "You can use body and speech to evoke beings' power"; and "As all things are mind, one may as well laugh loudly"—all have hinted at the boundless spiritual wealth of the Buddhist accomplishers.[1] They point to the goal and ways of the Great Seal, and their skillful methods enable independent people to also help others. While avoiding intellectual and emotional pitfalls, the resultant insights confirm both what is relative (the way) and what is absolute (the goal) as being in essence joyful. Among the frequently moralistic or superficial offers presented on today's spiritual market, such teachings will exert a growing attraction.

Enlightenment is the full development of all the qualities and abilities of beings, including the indispensable faculty of reason. The steps towards this state cannot be airy-fairy or exotic, and seven hundred years ago the 3rd Karmapa knew this. Simply bathing in their artistic power or making numerous repetitions of the following psychologically effective twenty-five verses will not be sufficient. Without critical analysis, several levels of meaning will be recognized too slowly. Therefore I sometimes choose commentaries that are eye opening and confrontational to a world that is trying to stay blissfully unaware of difficult facts. The critical view thus developed sharpens the understanding of the text, which then

---

1. Accomplisher (Skt. *Yogi*)—a meditator who has realized the nature of mind.

bestows a mature overview of the world and the ability to handle daily situations.

Every development in Buddhism starts from a critical analysis of the current situation. This allows one to understand, in an unshakable way, that the present moment offers the most precious and amazingly rare conditions and that one can actually steer one's life consciously towards liberation and enlightenment. These insights are generally known as the "Four Basic Thoughts."

We must first recognize that only very few people around the world have the chance to meet Buddha's full teachings from an educated, free, and empowered position and that only a fraction of them actually use this opportunity.

The second understanding focuses on the impermanence of everything outer and inner. One may die at any moment and only the space-awareness of mind is present always and everywhere. This makes mind vitally important, and we recognize the reasons for practicing here and now.

The third observation centers on cause and effect (Skt. *karma*, Tib. *lae*). In each moment, beings' thoughts, words, and actions lay the seeds for their future. As the results will have the same emotional color as their cause, it pays to be attentive.

Finally, we understand the wisdom of common growth. It becomes increasingly evident that all beings aim for transient kinds of happiness while trying to avoid suffering. Enlightenment, however, is the most formidable happiness of all and can neither disappear nor dissolve. Closing one's mind to its richest potential through laziness or a lack of imagination would be a grievous mistake. Whoever remains on a conceptual level where one experiences being one's body and owning one's possessions does not have the power to ultimately benefit others and finds little comfort when old age, sickness, death, and loss arrive.

These four thoughts give rise to a search for values that can be trusted. Here, only space has the quality of being indestructible, everywhere and always. Though frequently misunderstood by the immature to be a "nothing" or something missing, space is clearly no vacuous black hole. It is much more like a container that holds, communicates among, and makes all beings and events possible. Its essence is immediate intuitive insight; its nature is playful joy; and its expression is active compassion, which benefits beings. It manifests in peace-giving, enriching, fascinating, and powerfully protective ways. Shunning the politically correct, it aims to bring lasting benefit to cultures and beings.

Disturbing feelings, taken seriously by so many, are transformed on the way to enlightenment and become mirror-like, equalizing, discriminating, experiential, and all-pervading wisdoms.[2] As Buddha—or *Sangye* in Tibetan—embodies these levels, activities, and qualities, his state is the first and absolute refuge.

The second rare and precious refuge are the methods bringing beings to this state. Called *dharma* in Sanskrit and *choe* in Tibetan, Buddha's teachings consist of 84,000 methods. Filling 108 inch-thick books, they make it possible to advance at the desired speed.

The third refuge, *sangha* in Sanskrit and in Tibetan *gendun*, are one's friends on the way, especially the people who see life as a dream and have the strong wish to benefit others, those we call bodhisattvas. Each Diamond Way Buddhist center surely has noble women and men on this level.

If we want to use the exceedingly fast Diamond Way, a fourth refuge becomes necessary. It unites the former three and anchors them in life. This is the teacher, formerly known as *guru* in Sanskrit or *lama* in Tibetan. To avoid confusion or

---

2. See also Lama Ole Nydahl, *The Way Things Are*. (Nevada City, CA: Blue Dolphin, 1996; UK: O Books, 2008).

rumors, he (or she) must live in a monastery as a monk (or nun), function as a layperson, or have the enlightened view of an accomplisher. He must keep his outer vows, inner promises, and personal bonds; have life-experience; and represent Buddha's body, speech, and mind in a meaningful way. In the Diamond Way, his ability to bring confidence or blessing is particularly important. He must have a real transmission into and experience of the special methods of the ways with and without form—such as the yidam meditations, deep breathing exercises, and the Great Seal or Great Perfection teachings. He must also be surrounded by a field of enlightened protectors. The latter will also extend to his students and make their every experience a step on their way.

The lama, yidams, and wisdom protectors are also called the "three roots of accomplishment." The lama gives blessing, the conviction that great goals can be reached and that things are meaningful. The yidams give spiritual powers and the wisdom protectors are the source of one's power to act. Sometimes mentioned singly and sometimes collectively as "lama," these three are essential for progress on the Diamond Way.

Before 1992, when so many Tibetan "venerabilities" of the usually independent Karma Kagyu school dove into the Communist Chinese honey-pot, one still spoke of "high" and "ordinary" teachers. This is now over. The ensuing scandal forced the lineage to transform into an advanced Western transmission of the Diamond Way. So now everybody must take the trouble to imagine their teachers without any cultural packaging or exotic makeup. The students must decide for themselves if the lamas they trust do and say the same thing and if one can use their example for one's own life. As robes and rituals have lost much of their magic, people now evaluate what practical benefit a given teacher may bring them. Knowing that he cannot give what he does not have, they check if they can trust him or if they simply feel sympathy and like his explanations.

In the "Small Way" or "Words of the Elders of the Order"—the literal translation of the term *Theravada,* which is also known as *Hinayana* or Southern Buddhism—most take refuge to end or limit their own suffering. The meaning of this act increases immensely however, if one has the "Great Way" or *Mahayana* motivation of Northern Buddhism to develop quickly so one can benefit others. Driven by this strong wish, special qualities arise; and one can begin to balance mind's growing compassion and wisdom. From here, one may approach the amazing methods and views of the Diamond Way.

The above transference of one's values from what is conditioned and relative to the level of the absolute and timeless is the second necessary step on Buddha's way; a true refuge secures mind's future development and from here on one builds on this solid basis.

After deciding that one is attracted to the Diamond Way, two approaches appear. Some can mobilize the massive amounts of time and energy needed to enter directly into the Four Foundational Practices, the so-called *Ngondro.*[3] Others prefer to visit their local centers, find some time for meditation, increasingly hold Buddhist views and fit occasional courses into their yearly schedules. Both approaches are good and as soon as a certain degree of maturity has been reached, three ways open to those who have completed the Foundational Practices and two to those who have not. They build on the qualities inherent in mind and utilize its ability to know, to do, and to be inspired.

The first of these, the Way of Methods, was brought across the mountains to Tibet around 950 years ago by the hero

3. Lama Ole Nydahl, *Ngöndro.* (Nevada City, CA: Blue Dolphin, 1999).

Marpa. He received it from the accomplisher Naropa while the Muslim invaders were destroying the culture and freedom of northern India. With its focus on deep breathing and the energy channels in the body, it can only be used after the Foundational Practices. However, some of these meditations have limited relevance today as they require year-long preparations, which the Tibetan economic system permitted but are impossible for people who are today active in modern life. The Westerners who wish to enter extended and mostly celibate retreats are often already absorbed by their own affairs, and this tendency rarely changes afterwards. In addition to this, most of the practices are classified as secret and are not generally available. Except for the Phowa and Clear Light meditations—teachings for conscious dying and pervasive awareness—it is not possible to teach the Way of Methods to unprepared people with a clear conscience. Too many bodily and mental hindrances may ensue. Those who ignore this and teach them anyway, like some Rinpoches—often of other lineages—who have published these teachings, do not benefit themselves and may only help their students for a short period. The hurt pride, which follows failed attempts to use overly advanced meditations, may hinder one's approach to the Diamond Way in future lives.

Among the meditations of Tantric Buddhism, another name for the Way of Methods, the greatly desired union practices in particular call for years of absorption, very special partners, and long retreats. On the other hand, using one's body to consciously give joy to one's loved ones is a fine practice in its right. And if the good conditions come together to have a full and lasting experience of space as essential bliss, then one actually achieves the complete unfolding of mind, the state of the Great Seal.

The second approach, the Way of Insight, was the gift of Marpa's other main teacher, Maitripa. Though less engulfed in mystery, his conceptual and total methods are more useful in today's world. When calming and holding mind, the oneness and interdependence of subject, object, and action become clear—and intuitive insight arises. Some teachers give unstructured meditation of this kind right after refuge, teaching people to "simply" meditate on mind. I consider this a big mistake. The very fact that this way is so easy to describe makes it prone to misunderstanding. Any spiritual progress necessitates a wide framework of teachings and is only useful with the right guidance and a massive accumulation of good impressions as one's basis. Otherwise, mind's spontaneity easily degenerates into evaluating passing thoughts; and its shiny quality becomes a sleepy white wall. For that reason, in the meditation lineages of Tibet, such teachings were not given until the Foundational Practices were completed. It is actually much more difficult to calm and clear one's mind without methods than it is to acquaint oneself with the main Buddha-forms and learn their sometimes long and unusual sounding mantras.

The power of Maitripa's teaching lies in its versatility. Based on a pleasant exchange with one's surroundings, the methods require no strict retreats and are easily incorporated into one's lifestyle.

The first part of the Way of Insight called *shi-n*e in Tibetan or *shamata* in Sanskrit, calms and holds mind. All religions of experience—such as Buddhism, Taoism, and parts of Hinduism—strive for this state through varying means. This source of extrasensory perception and miracles may also be reached through prayer by members of the faith religions. Almost any method may be used on the Way of Insight to settle and focus mind. Some schools work with mental images, others avoid them. Some calm their mind through a slow, stork-like ritual walk or while chewing their food countless times. The one most commonly used in the "Words of the Elders of the Order" or *Theravada*, is to count the breath or to have an awareness of its passing at one's nostrils. The Great Way or Mahayana includes strong wishes for all beings or focuses on recognizing the interdependent origination and fundamental "emptiness" of all phenomena. If the latter understanding is experienced and not only "thought," this insight is called *lhagtong* in Tibetan or *vipashyana* in Sanskrit, the second part of the Way of Insight, and points directly to mind's essence.

To those with confidence in their buddha nature, the building-up phase in a Diamond Way meditation, called *Kye Rim* in Tibetan—which means the birth phase of the buddha aspect—is the most effective kind of shi-ne. Here, body, speech, and mind receive the feedback of the hologram-like figures of light and energy called *yidams;* of their natural vibrations, also known as mantras; and their experience of space and joy as inseparable. Whether a clear image appears or one simply senses the form and knows that enlightenment is wherever one thinks of it, the better one knows the qualities of a given buddha aspect and the stronger one wishes to obtain them, the more the transfer actually occurs. The experience of such pure forms, female or male, peaceful or protective, single or united, and the ensuing confidence from the energy and blessing experienced, has a total and profound effect. Their heart-vibrations (Skt. *mantra,* Tib. *ngag*) and the transformation of one's inner and outer world into their perfect wisdoms and pure lands influence body, speech, and all levels of mind concurrently.

Yidam meditations bring countless enlightened mirrors to mind's recognition of its own clarity, compassion, and wisdom. The bliss and thankfulness arising when melting together with the buddha aspects, as an expression of one's lama and through the dissolution of all form into timeless, limitless but information-holding space, will burn countless veils in one's mind. Sooner or later it will bring forth an all-encompassing consciousness. The resulting state of radiant awareness beyond concept or form is called *dzog rim* or the completion phase. It corresponds to the second step on Maitripa's way. To make the final step to the level of the Great Seal, one needs to realize that the meditator, the Buddha meditated upon and meditation itself—subject, object, and action—are all aspects of the same totality. This insight will fully open mind's potential and bring enlightenment.

The third and broadest approach to enlightenment—the Way of Identification with one's teacher—unites and blesses the described ways of methods and insight. This method is meaningful in all situations of life and 950 years ago Marpa's teacher, Naropa, described its effects as comparable to meditating on ten thousand yidam-forms of energy and light. It utilizes all of mind's qualities and is nourished by one's potential for enthusiastic intuition. Its power to widen mind's confidence in the teacher as the expression of one's inherent potential brings the fastest results. This approach of identification may actually be listed as an entirely independent way only because our main teacher, the 16th Karmapa Ranjung Rigpe Dorje gave it to Hannah and me in this format. Until recently, when some texts were discovered in Tibet and smuggled out, nobody was apparently aware that former Karmapas had done exactly the same. It is known as *lami naljor* in Tibetan or *guru yoga* in Sanskrit and has always been the secret transformative power of the Kagyu lineage. More than ever, it is the cornerstone of the idealistic new Diamond Way groups in the West. Meditations on one's closest lama and the 16th Karmapa as inseparable from one's mind and as mirrors showing one's potential help more students open up to the blessing of the lineage than any other practice today. Devotion, however, should always be combined with human maturity. Confidence in the teacher must never lead to dependency, humorless behavior, or compulsive imitation. The damage brought about by such tendencies is made evident by the frequent scandals in charismatic cults and sects. A lama only has one role to fulfill: helping his students to find the fearless space that he himself has conquered, thus making them independent. Within the freedom of unfiltered consciousness, one discovers the perfect qualities that were always present in all worlds and in everyone's mind.

The development of awareness, energy, and identification described above should be grounded in the view of the Great Seal as soon as possible. They should then be developed through the four levels of this absolute realization and carried to its ultimate fruit. One insight alone transforms each event into an enlightening experience: the interdependence of subject, object, and action. This highest view allows everybody to be close to life and responsible at the same time. Real maturity means being far-sighted and fulfilling the actual needs of beings by working with causes rather than, short-sightedly, catering to their superficial and changing wishes. Whoever can see the world as the flow of private dreams inside a large collective one, which it truly is, has no option but to work compassionately for the good of all beings.

Thus, it makes no difference if one uses calming meditations to enable mind's limitless wisdom to appear, driven by the feeling that space is joy, or if thankful devotion and confidence in one's enlightened nature motivate one on the Way of Identification: Each way leads to enlightenment, the fruit of the Great Seal.

While teaching in a German castle in the eighties, Kunzig Shamarpa once said that the 16th Karmapa was unable to transmit his one-step way to enlightenment because the times were simply too crazy. The approach consisting of four steps, however, is today open to whoever creates the necessary circumstances. Although the 3rd Karmapa does not use this classification in his twenty-five verses, for the sake of the widest possible view it should be included here.

Uniting basis, way, and goal, the first level is called "one-pointedness." This describes a state where mind enjoys what is there. It is so filled with good impressions that it needs nothing from anywhere else.

Then follows the state of being "non-artificial." Here, one naturally stops pretending, playing games, or behaving superficially. As the uniqueness of everything is so evidently rich and evident, everything artificial falls away.

At the third stage there follows "one taste." This is where the experiencer becomes conscious of itself behind the flow of experiences and mind's timeless mirror recognizes its radiant essence underneath the images it reflects. Non-meditators may also experience this state sometimes where mind is open and totally aware. The search of so many for excitement shows the importance and greatness of self-arisen joy. Once obtained, on the inner and secret levels, it radiates through every conditioned experience and is never again lost.

The last and ultimate state was given a name that is actually a joke. As its essence is highest fulfillment, where the universe vibrates with laughter, it cannot be described with a serious face. Called "non-meditation," it actually means to be without effort, because there is nothing further to be obtained. Here the intensity of ten thousand volts is felt in every cell of one's body and one works ceaselessly for others without even thinking "I" do something for "you." Beyond our ordinary senses, we experience mind through the vibration of each atom.

Thus having become a buddha, no separation in time or space is limiting or real. We act from mind's omniscience and benefit beings in a lasting way, here and now. Thus all things become meaningful. Everything is mind's free play. Every being is recognized to be a buddha who only needs to discover his essence and the world is actually a pure land. This is real enlightenment, the state of the Great Seal.

The following twenty-five verses of the *Chag Chen Monlam* composed by the 3rd Karmapa Rangjung Dorje seven hundred years ago may be read independently of other sources. They point to the nature of mind and are therefore rare and precious.

Yours,

Lama Ole

༄༅། །དེས་དོན་ཕྱག་རྒྱ་ཆེན་པོའི་སྨོན་ལམ་
ཞེས་བྱ་བ་རྗེ་རང་བྱུང་རྡོ་རྗེས་མཛད་པའོ། ། །

བླ་མ་རྣམས་དང་ཡི་དམ་དཀྱིལ་འཁོར་ལྷ། །

Lamas and buddhas of the yidam powerfields, buddhas

ཕྱོགས་བཅུ་དུས་གསུམ་རྒྱལ་བ་སྲས་དང་བཅས། །

and bodhisattvas of the three times and ten directions, think lovingly of us.

བདག་ལ་བརྩེར་དགོངས་བདག་གི་སྨོན་ལམ་རྣམས། །

Please give your blessing that our wishes may be

ཇི་བཞིན་འགྲུབ་པའི་མཐུན་འགྱུར་བྱིན་བརླབས་མཛོད། །

fulfilled the way that they are made.

Verse 1

For something to grow, the first necessity is a field. Then seeds, sun, and rain must be added. Only then is a harvest possible. Reaching enlightenment is a similar process, and in this first verse Karmapa assembles the necessary powerfield. All Buddha's teachings and meditations start with refuge in the full expression of mind. As this state is the goal, it should be understood at the beginning of his wishes. Without the first rung on a ladder the remainder have little meaning. What then can be a lasting refuge? First, there are the three "rare and precious ones" or "jewels": the buddha, his teaching, and the bodhisattvas, one's friends on the way. Similarly important on the Diamond Way are the three "roots" of one's development: one's lama, the yidams, and the protectors.

Buddhas are not gods; they neither judge, punish, nor create but are the friends of beings. Feeling no separation in time and space, they are all knowing and fully enlightened. In Sanskrit, buddha means "awakened"; and the translation that the Tibetans chose, *san-gye*, expresses the two qualities of being "without any veil" and "fully matured." Buddhahood may be summarized by three states, four activities, and five wisdoms. The text will return to these points several times and there are more detailed explanations in my book *The Way Things Are*. For now, they will just be mentioned briefly.

The three states are those of enlightened fearless wisdom, self-arisen bliss, and far-sighted, meaningful action. They appear spontaneously from the experience of mind as indestructible space, luminously clear and limitless, and let the four fields of activity arise. Working in peace-giving, enriching, fascinating and protective ways, the Buddhas benefit beings. When disturbing feelings are recognized as meaningless and allowed to return to space having not been acted upon, liberating intuition appears in their place. Thus, an enlightened mind manifests mirror-like, equalizing, discriminating, experiential, and intuitive, all-pervading wisdoms.

Buddha's teachings are inseparable from him; they are his life, his work, and his activity. These multipurpose tools for benefiting beings—84,000 instructions and pieces of advice filling 108 inch-thick books—have brought people to the full development of their potential over the last 2,550 years. The vastness of the teachings, however, is no reason to avoid Buddhism. Although a lama should be able to deal with many different needs, in general, each individual should know only what fits his or her situation. A good restaurant has a long menu!

Becoming a bodhisattva is the provisional goal of Northern or Great Way Buddhism. On this level of insight, the illusion of a real "self" or "I" has been dissolved, but the veil of limiting views has not. Therefore, one can still make mistakes but will never fall out of this state. Expressing the rich qualities of power, wisdom, and love, bodhisattvas have an increasing ability to benefit beings while they themselves are developing.

The invocation of the lamas and the yidams' powerfields shows that Karmapa intends to transmit something that is beyond concepts. This is the preparation for a Diamond Way text. All Buddhist schools use the outer refuge of the aforementioned three jewels, which are known in Sanskrit as *buddha, dharma, and sangha.* In our case, however, the aim is the absolute experience of the Great Seal works on all levels with the potential of body, speech, and mind. Here, a close and instant refuge, the "three roots"—of immediate realization are essential. They supply the necessary frame for one's total development. With his first stanza, Karmapa Rangjung Dorje invokes the most potent and beneficial forces for his readers.

How should these three roots be understood? As there is no difference between the truth concerning the inside (one's mental patterns) and that of the outside (all worldly phenomena), they cannot be anything but extremely effective mirrors to the power of one's mind.

From the teacher one obtains that for which the best term may still be "blessing." This may be a blissful, inner warmth, a feeling of being charged up, the disappearance of one's questions or an ever-increasing confidence that an absolute goal is reachable. If the lama has not yet become unshakable, he must at least be able to represent the refuge through some other less reliable qualities such as a well-founded knowledge of the texts and a behavior that people can identify with. Being the "Root of Accomplishment," he is as irreplaceable as the groups and centers that hold his energy field. Anyone can learn to walk or run; but if one wants to fly, one needs a teacher. Although it is often stated that practitioners will obtain their teacher's qualities, in Buddhism—and especially the perpetually new and refreshing methods of the Diamond Way—they skillfully prevent the danger of becoming their clone. The reason that a lama and a student bond is that, on a deep level, they naturally share some basic affinities; but nobody should be stretched or squeezed to conform to a particular model. A fitting analogy would be that of entering a beautiful hall of mirrors created by the teacher's fearlessness. In his powerfield, one's natural qualities are convincingly discovered (see verse 4).

Yidam, the "Root of Methods," brings highly effective means to the direct recognition of mind. Many already know the colorful buddha aspects, which appear like holographic figures of energy and light. Peace-giving or protective, single or united, female or male, they mirror beings' inherent enlightened qualities of body, speech, and mind—making it easier to realize them oneself. The view of the Great Seal, as well as the phases of melting together with the buddhas of energy and light, are some of the most effective methods available. Any involvement with them brings about beyond-personal feedback, which is like recognizing one's features more clearly each time one looks in a mirror. No more complete methods for accomplishing courage, bliss, and intelligent compassion exist. The Tibetan term expresses everything: *yi* means mind and *dam* bond. Such transmissions empower mind to recognize its buddha nature.

Whoever manages to reach the level of buddhahood and enlightenment will be constantly surrounded by the energy fields of these light forms. In Sanskrit the word is *mandala* and in Tibetan *kyilkhor*, which means "the center and what is around." These buddhas are frequently depicted, either in sand or painted, as the floor plan or aerial view of a palace. Expressing thirty-two perfect qualities, which manifest from the level of liberation and reach full maturity at enlightenment, these energy fields condense around them as wish-fulfilling palaces of light. If the Buddhas express peaceful qualities, these structures are square and have rainbow-colored walls. For more forceful expressions the energy fields will be darker and triangular. In essence, all are pure and transparent and surrounded by the powerful protectors, the "Root of Activity." Although, because of their complexity, they are rarely shown on the ritual Tibetan scrolls *(thangkas)* or mentioned in the meditations, they are neither abstract nor from another world. Also, when buddhas function as yidams, even a short or partial experience of their power is unforgettable and changes one's life.

Nothing works in a lasting way without the "wisdom protectors." They give the power to act. Inseparable from the lama, they appear instantaneously in all situations of life during a meditation, in order to protect those whom they can reach. In spite of their exciting appearance, their weapons and the flames around them, any protector with an additional vertical wisdom-eye in the forehead is completely without disturbing feelings. Knowing neither ill will nor anger, they express themselves powerfully to liberate beings from obstacles. In contrast to unenlightened energy fields, they do not postpone unpleasant karmic results but give the strength to remove their causes. This is the reason for their Tibetan name, *yeshe goenpo:* "protector through highest wisdom." These helpful energies turn the kind of trouble in peoples' inner life, which they would otherwise not be able to learn from, into minor accidents, difficulties, and diseases. They also ensure that those difficult experiences, which one can handle and learn from on one's way will surface from one's store-consciousness at the right time and place. In the outer world, the protectors often work in an immediate and very visible manner. They either keep at bay accidents and other hindrances to one's life and development or at least weaken their impact.

Each of the enlightened forces invoked and the refuge in its totality work in this way. Like hooks catching a ring, they reach into the conditioned world and help whoever has opened up to them. Their all-pervading activity covers the **"ten directions"** (zenith, nadir, the main and the intermediary points of the compass), and they bless the **"three times"**— (past, present, and future).

Karmapa's last words may bother an idealistic Westerner, whose confidence in his teacher and his own mind may have taken some effort to establish. It is not easy to understand why he adds that the refuge may carry out these wishes **"the**

way that they are made." This must have been a concession to his less adept students, i.e., to that majority who seven hundred years ago had not received an education and thus had little chance of grasping abstract concepts. If no beyond-personal view has been established and there is no real understanding of cause and effect or Karma, things remain very personal. Passing joy and pain are felt to be very lasting. One sees them as coming from outside sources and looks for protection from what seems to be uncontrollable. These wishes allow one to worry less about problematic conditions and instead to open up with more confidence to a world that is not yet easily understood.

Thus, this whole first verse is an introduction. For the benefit of his students, Karmapa brings all of enlightenment to their side. This prepares the ground for the growth that will follow.

The historical Shakyamuni Buddha

བདག་དང་མཐའ་ཡས་སེམས་ཅན་ཐམས་ཅད་ཀྱི། །

Sprung from the snowy mountain of our perfectly pure

བསམ་སྦྱོར་རྣམ་དག་གངས་རི་ལས་སྐྱེས་པའི། །

intentions and actions and those of all beings, may the

ལབར་གསུམ་ཉག་མད་དག་ཆགས་རྒྱ་རྒྱུན་རྣམས། །

stream of all good deeds empty into the ocean of the

རྒྱལ་བ་སྐུ་བཞིའི་རྒྱ་མཚོར་འཇུག་གྱུར་ཅིག །

four buddha states, without the mud of the three concepts.

VERSE 2

After the praise, refuge, and invocation of the first verse, the imagery that now follows is set in the natural world. It is enjoyable and easily understandable but at the same time thought provoking. These lines express the wish that the **"stream of all good deeds . . . from the snowy mountain of our perfectly pure intentions and actions"** will reach its goal, that it may meet no obstacle on its way to the ocean of the **Four Buddha States.**

The opponents on this path are not one-hundred-pound weaklings but the source of all suffering. Nothing other than these **"three concepts"** brings beings' naturally perfect, free, and blissful mind to feel pain. They are the superficial perception of a separation between experiencer, experience, and object experienced; and the success of one's life depends on the degree to which one manages to dissolve them.

The origin of these concepts is the tendency of any unenlightened mind to function like an eye. It experiences what appears but not itself and therefore does not recognize its own all-encompassing space. The inability to understand that it is essentially mind's all-pervading consciousness is the cause of all hindrances. Although nothing lasting or real can be found in either the body or one's thoughts, because of this basic ignorance, space that is aware experiences itself as an "I." Thereby its clarity and richness, which produce the inner and outer worlds, becomes a "you" or something "separate." The interaction between the "I" and the "you" results in the disturbing feelings, which are taken to be real and later lead to clumsy words and actions. Then the feedback from one's store-consciousness and the outer world again produce unpleasant experiences, which strengthen one's tendency towards further unskillful acts. Although they are mainly felt as fluctuating levels of adrenaline that one only gradually learns to control, these disturbing feelings are still taken as one's basis for action and cause the suffering of all beings that are not liberated. Therefore, very few experience just how embarrassing anger is and that it is a certain sign of weakness. Genuinely strong people feel no frustration. They can simply do what they want.

Karmapa is acutely aware of this point and continues to bring it up throughout the remaining verses. The inability to recognize the interdependence of experiencer, object experienced, and act of experiencing is nothing trivial. Although one would not predict an enlightened teacher to invoke images like that of "mud," they are actually an essential understatement. If one's mind has great power, one must be kind; otherwise the damage done is too vast. Whoever has only handguns can go to war while those with nuclear weapons must remain peaceful. Danes have a saying, "little dogs bark, big ones don't need to"; and the strongest statement that the 16th Karmapa ever made in the presence of Hannah and myself was: "You must be careful." Later that night I ended up pushing a broken-down car through parts of Harlem where it was unhealthy to show a white face. Simply stated, Karmapa advises one to stay aware of mind's fundamental freedom. Before delving into the limited views of the three concepts or accepting the "either-or" view they restrict one to, one should carefully consider if these are experiences one wants or needs.

To impart an understanding of the Four Buddha States, as a knower of mind Karmapa frequently gives enlightened overviews. The basis for mind's full expression is usually compared to humidity but here, it is symbolized by snow—it is the truth-state. Formerly it was known as the *dharmakaya* (Skt.) or *choeku* (Tib.). In this state, space is information. It is neither an unconscious black hole nor something missing. Instead, space is a container bringing forth, knowing, encompassing, and uniting. All things depend upon and influence one another. However large separating distances may be, there is always more space behind the objects than between them.

Truth is all-pervading. It is the vibration of each particle, every appearance and disappearance, beings' birth and death. The fact that all phenomena ultimately appear from the potential of space and have causes on the relative level makes them basically true. Whether or not this pleases dependent individuals, all objects, people, and events need neither an outside creating entity nor any kind of approval from elsewhere. Inseparable from maturity and intuitive wisdom, this understanding brings about the state of fearlessness, the basis for all fine qualities. It manifests effortlessly when mind recognizes its indestructible space-nature.

The rich potential of space, its free play, clarity, and constant freshness is called the joy-state, *sambhogakaya* (Skt.) or *longku* (Tib.) In this context it is the stream. This state manifests outside as the yidam powerfields of energy and light and inside as immediate experiences of recognition, artistic expression, and purity. There is always something going on; outer and inner events change in every instant. Experiencing this richness with complete awareness is mind's self-arisen highest bliss. This second aspect of buddhahood where mind fearlessly discovers its rich potential and strength needs no other cause than this. Being unchanging like a mirror or the depth of the ocean, instead of being conditioned like images and waves, the joy-state appears when nothing is expected or feared. This blissful space-awareness, which is nothing but mind's radiance, will manifest wherever conditions permit.

A third richness coexists with one's insight into mind's essential space, the interdependent functioning of all things and the bliss of experiencing mind's clarity. It is the activity state, *nirmanakaya* (Skt.) or *tulku* (Tib.). Karmapa here uses an ocean to symbolize this state, which also has no other cause than mind. It relies on the recognition that the experiencer is basically unobstructed and unlimited. In spite of the marked differences in people's tendencies towards abstract thinking and in their needs to understand the causes and effects of their worlds, all want nothing but happiness and also ultimately share the same inner and outer space. When this is understood, one must benefit beings in an intelligent, foreseeing way. In today's world that would mean above all else to enable poor people to have fewer children and to educate the ones they have. This ocean of compassionate actions targets the sources of suffering. It springs from the unlimited qualities of mind and expresses itself through the four so-called buddha activities.

Depending on the cultural circumstances this wisdom and compassion may express itself as incarnate Buddhist teachers, like the famous Gyalwa Karmapas, including Thaye Dorje who now lives in Kalimpong, India, and the Kunzig Sharmapas of the Karma Kagyu Lineage. It is also active as the many officially unrecognized Western idealists who can get closer to people by not using a title or wearing robes. In both cases, their work will never succeed unless they have a genuine transmission, have a clear head, truly like others, and have real life-experience.

Truth, bliss, and intelligent action—what could be added to these three perfections? Only its essence, the ultimate state. If "space as information" (truth) is compared to water-vapor, all-pervading but invisible, "space as spontaneous play" (bliss) would be the clouds that appear there and "space as meaningful action" (compassion) would be the rain that makes things grow. In spite of the perceived differences, they are all water. This then is like the fourth, Essential State, *Svabhavikakaya* (Skt.) and *Ngowonyigiku* (Tib.). Together, these four states are a perfectly functioning mind.

The Four Buddha States

	Truth-State	Joy-State	Active-compassionate State	Essence-State
Sanskrit	Dharmakaya	Sambhogakaya	Nirmanakaya	Svabhavikakaya
Tibetan	Choeku	Longku	Tulku	Ngowonyigiku
Realization	Fearlessness	Joy	Love	Equanimity
View	Timeless space	Playful richness	Limitlessness	Resting effortlessly
Comparison	Water vapor	Clouds	Rain	Water

ཇི་སྲིད་དེ་མ་ཐོབ་པ་དེ་སྲིད་དུ། །

As long as this has not yet been accomplished,

སྐྱེ་དང་སྐྱེ་བ་ཚེ་རབས་ཀུན་ཏུ་ཡང་། །

during this and in all future lives,

སྡིག་དང་སྡུག་བསྔལ་སྒྲ་ཡང་མི་གྲག་ཅིང་། །

may we not even hear words like evil and pain,

བདེ་དགེ་རྒྱ་མཚོའི་དཔལ་ལ་སྤྱོད་པར་ཤོག །

but instead experience oceans of goodness and bliss.

VERSE 3

In this verse most of the meaning is written between the lines. It can appear quite foreign to the northern European view of "big enemy, great honor" that has now spread across the Western world. In Asian cultures nobody except for a few wild yogis would climb the highest mountains just to see how it feels or if one can do it. Such societies prefer a kind of conformist behavior that seems precocious to Westerners and often embarrasses them, while to age-old, conservative cultures Western pushiness and transparency appear uncivilized. Only recently have Far East Asians tried the Western way of growing through experiences on the edge of life, and these cultures thus draw closer. The distance that has remained, however, is aptly exemplified by the degree of incomprehension we have towards what is a grave Chinese curse, "May you live in interesting times." To us, this would suggest periods of transformation, excitement, and upheaval—the outer frame for a potentially fulfilling life. To older ways of thinking, this would imply that the divine order of the universe was seriously unbalanced.

With his statements, the 3rd Karmapa seems to satisfy this inclination towards a quiet, well-ordered world. This would probably be in the vein of the tamed Central Tibetans who were used to being regulated by three vast monasteries but would be far too uneventful for an East Tibetan Khampa warrior. Instead of proposing a quick recognition of one's own face through the destruction of all limits and concepts, his wishes seem to go towards a protected approach with steady growth, a way with a minimum of difficulties.

If one has had no experience of the accomplished or "yogi" level of bliss and power, which is the source of his words, then one could easily take these words to have the feeling of wanting to avoid life. In the given context however, this view is not relevant. Karmapa here points to states that are beyond differing cultures and temperaments and are inherent in mind beyond any limitation in time and place. The subject of his words is the Great Seal, the Maha-mudra. Completely beyond any concept of running away or hiding from life, this verse points to the highest, liberating bliss and freedom, that of mind's natural state. It spontaneously brings about everything meaningful and effortless and aims to show the reader what is absolute. In and behind the conditioned, it transmits a first taste of the luminosity of the mirror behind its pictures. Whoever feels the timeless radiance of the experiencer will no longer be disturbed by his own difficulties or suffering. Without sentimentality or self-pity, he recognizes them to be faulty programs and removes their causes at his leisure.

From where do conditioned experiences arise? From cause and effect (Skt. *karma,* Tib. *lae).* All events are caused by stored mental impressions. Sour people clash with similarly difficult cases while joyful people easily find pleasant companions. One attracts what one radiates into the world. Heaven and hell happens between one's ears, ribs, or wherever else one imagines one's mind to reside. However strange one's inner Disneyland may present itself, nothing can change the essence of experiences. Luminous space, the aware potential for everything and its clarity, which makes outer and inner worlds appear, is in its very nature absolute and unchangeable. Whoever experiences the experiencer in its totality and not only through words and concepts will additionally know it to be unlimited. Below the waves there is always the depth of the ocean (see verse 2). From one's entry into the levels of the Great Seal a deep conviction grows that this is true. One now knows for sure that an indestructible experiencer exists. From the state of "one taste" and on, this recognition remains. For this reason the statements in this verse are not a willful avoidance of facts in order to see only beauty. By wishing one **"oceans of goodness and bliss,"** Karmapa does not intend to shield one from life and the chance to mature. However, joy and fulfillment possess a higher level of truth than evil and suffering. They are lasting and supply certain essential ingredients for enlightenment.

Such feelings of surplus express a limitless potential for richness and are not a passing fad. One thus acts with increasing effectiveness for others. When habitual veils dissolve, one sees with increasing precision what is relevant and becomes more decisive in what one does.

Thus a "pure view" does not mean shirking away from confrontation. Instead, acting in a beyond-personal way without disturbing feelings, one responsibly works for what will most benefit the world as far into the future as one can see. This is essential, especially when it requires rolling up one's sleeves or disturbing politically correct people. Not preventing future suffering because of sentimentality or a lack of courage in facing facts is the deepest breach of confidence. For example, on the practical level of today's politics, allowing slums to appear for foreigners who do not feel at home in their host countries is bringing increasing trouble. Helping these people in a lasting way by a functioning system of educated contraception has long been the obvious solution.

Blind compassion is harmful; and even with the finest inclination to benefit beings, one should use one's intelligence and look generations ahead. People who can rest in themselves and the world from an unshakable center will act in the right way and when the time is ripe. In contrast to faith religions, suffering is nothing heroic in Buddhism. It is a sign that one has made a mistake. Whatever trouble one goes through for the benefit of others does not feel painful but is fulfilling and joyful instead.

The finest and only timeless gift, which one can give others, is the certainty that highest bliss is highest truth. If in addition one manages to skillfully inform people about causality, one has given them the key to real happiness.

The insight that one can only awaken to liberation and happiness from a good dream, while any harmful behavior brings additional difficulties, skillfully unites what is relative and absolute.

Saraha

དལ་འབྱོར་མཆོག་ག་ཐོབ་དང་བརྟེན་ཤེས་རབ་ལྡན། །

Having obtained excellent freedoms and endowments, as well as

བཞེས་གཉེན་བཟང་བསྟེན་གདམས་པའི་བཅུད་ཐོབ་ནར

confidence, diligence, and insight—as a result of having been sustained by

ཚུལ་བཞིན་བསྒྲུབ་ལ་བར་ཆད་མ་མཆིས་པར། །

a spiritual teacher and receiving his essential instructions—may we

ཚེ་རབས་ཀུན་ཏུ་དམ་ཆོས་སྒྲུད་པར་ཤོག། །

correctly follow them without hindrance, realize them, and practice the noble teachings in all future lives.

VERSE 4

At first glance, the subject matter of this verse comes across as somewhat forthright and makes few hearts race. It does however contain essential Buddhist teachings concerning the "precious human life," which are considered even today, at the start of every Diamond Way meditation. Distractions and habits are strong, and life can easily flow by with little lasting meaning. Only those who employ the antidote of remembering their freedoms and possibilities will effectively obtain timeless goals.

What do the first lines actually say? That at present we have the possibility to move towards liberation and enlightenment. Many factors—**"freedoms and endowments"**—have come together for us to not just grow older, like everyone else, but also wiser. This is nothing ordinary or self-evident! Today, probably 85 percent of the world's population live under conditions that make spiritual growth almost impossible. Even in the rich, free, and educated countries, which offer the opportunity, people's priorities are mostly immature. Few seek anything ultimate, and it is considered one's best investment to spend twenty years from the age of six at schools and universities. Unfortunately, it doesn't guarantee happiness; and earning more money during the following thirty to forty years helps nobody beyond the grave. Only a tiny fraction of the brightest people pick up the scent of the strongest and only lasting fulfillment, which has been inherent in all beings since beginningless time: the experience of mind. The conscious use of such conditions to find values that give meaning through old age, sickness, death, and rebirth is what makes a life precious.

The **"confidence"** mentioned above, in no way implies faith or believing in an outer entity separate from oneself. Neither does it mean accepting unwanted outside pressure, closing one's eyes to facts, nor swallowing any dogma sideways. Buddhism is a religion of experience, not of faith; and Buddha wanted aware colleagues, not blind followers. Buddhists develop with their teachers and friends, but on the basis of right understanding and self-reliance. Using meditations that have remained effective during thousands of years, a real experience of mind must appear.

It is actually possible to doubt one's way, at least up to the point of liberation. If one is wise enough to not always question the same things, but instead add each solved point to one's former insights, one will eventually arrive. However, the way is of course much faster if one can include the tested experiences of others. When way and goal are both deeply convincing and enlightenment comes into sight, then the accomplishing yogi can extend the antennas of his awareness completely and perform trusting leaps into mind's limitless and exciting realms.

"Diligence" means creative joy and enthusiastic activity. It feeds on the basically good feeling of recognizing new aspects of one's strengths. Enlarging the comfortable world that one already mastered into the somewhat cooler but unlimited space of untried possibilities is real growth. It is always joyful that something moves and unfolds. Among all one's accumulated qualities, the level of activity reached is most directly transmitted between one's lives. Therefore whoever measures himself by what he can or will not do in life, will probably have a body with little energy next time.

With today's flood of mixed and doctored information from so many sides, the most needed **"insight"** is the ability to discriminate. On the relative level, one must check what comes from where, who wants to peddle what, what the current environment and history of a situation is, and whether one should become involved in it or not. Especially in spiritual matters, way and goal of one's chosen approach must be understood and a clear realization has to be gained of what should not be mixed up under any circumstances. This is because both the methods and results of the world's religions are quite different and because similar terms may be used for different phenomena and vice versa. Leaving behind the religions of dogma and bone-hard contracts and joining those of the Far East, which aim to develop human beings, does not mean that one can forget about discrimination. The realm of free spirituality proves to be deeply vulnerable. This point is made evident by the dramatic and confused behavior of many self-appointed "enlightened" teachers who often claim to be above traditional religions. Critical observations and a readiness to laugh at the comical or artificial aspects of certain spiritual offers are an important safeguard of common sense. It is unfortunate that they seem to be rarely employed by some cultures where women are suppressed or other crimes against freedom frequently occur.

The spiritual teacher is hardly mentioned elsewhere in Karmapa's text, but a wide-reaching examination of their role is required. As a Buddhist, one should generally avoid strongly moralistic viewpoints. But, then, how does one approach with a critical intelligence the often idealized presentations of the spiritual teacher and the frequent scandals of super-rich gurus? Surely these dilemmas are not just a modern-day phenomena, so how is Karmapa's advice to be understood? Well, in the Eastern religions of experience and not of faith, there were well-known guidelines. In Buddhism, the relationship between teacher and student gave the teacher a clearly defined role; and their colleagues, competition or tutors checked their style. They ensured that it was difficult to get away with any self-concocted rituals, flashes of overly exotic behavior, or the use of pressure to extort money from susceptible people. Unfortunately, upon entering the unconstrained free space of the West, several lamas have produced opaque, cultural hierarchies; and only a few respected their students enough to avoid controlling them through fear. This is a major weakness that is probably shared with all other traditional religions. Today it disturbs and scares away the most powerful and independent people.

A general unwillingness by the press to critically examine the structures and religious, or should we say political, hierarchies of Tibet may ultimately destroy their chance to remain relevant. If one is never objectively analyzed but instead put in a museum among threatened and extinct cultures, then there is no chance for people to adapt and learn. Recurrent Buddhist scandals have proven this to be true. Even teachers who are reputed to have reached a beyond-personal or even self-liberating view may apparently still make massive and embarrassing mistakes on the practical level. Therefore, Western values like life-experience and a healthy resistance to authority are more indispensable than ever. Installing them should be a lama's first concern. The example one should set in Buddhism would be to think independently, speak from experience, and behave as one advises others to. Although few students are aware of it, the lama is in fact exceedingly free in his choice of methods to bring this maturity about. If he understands Buddha's ultimate teachings, has compassion, and works hard, a teacher may bring masses of good to others—and this is what Karmapa expresses here. The lama is the basis for the effective methods of the Diamond Way.

In spite of the embarrassment some teachers have caused—on the sexual and organizational front in the celibate orders and mainly due to a lack of information in the lay orders—the West has today come to the intelligent conclusion that their function must be kept alive. One simply learns best from those who are a convincing living example. Outer trimmings, like the robes and number of mattresses they sit on, have lost their exotic pull; and people are ever more aware that each member of a tradition must be individually and accurately examined.

The following additional points may facilitate one's understanding of the view of the teacher employed by the 3rd Karmapa and his contemporaries. Without this, the text could easily create cultural barriers or disturb informed people. Karmapa must have consciously chosen to introduce the spiritual teacher without any checks or pre-conditions. Seven hundred years ago, when these wishes were made, human relationships were not so different from today. Although the outer frame was stark and simple, there were also then plenty of "Rogues in Robes."[1] Tibet's history is full of spiritual authorities who misused their students' devotion or installed fear for personal gain. Probably in compensation for missing the joys of the night, members of monasteries frequently develop a wish for power and a strong sense of pride. The student is in fact only properly protected when they teach from a level of advanced human maturity and under a watchful public eye.

Making a productive human bond like this work is a complicated task and it is good to stay aware of one's motivation. Some choose their teacher because of his compliance with outer vows, and the status of a celibate monk or nun allows them to avoid areas of life where they may have been hurt

1. Tomek Lehnert, *Rogues in Robes.* (Nevada City, CA: Blue Dolphin, 1998).

or lack a pure view. However, this makes it difficult for the teacher to be a practical example on many levels of human expression, and if the students later want to change their lifestyles, the first teacher may do well to send them to other lamas in order to round off their capabilities.

If one builds the connection to one's teacher upon the bodhisattva promise as lay people do, learning depends more on the lama's activity. If he works hard, transparently and with intelligence for the benefit of people, the range of exchange may be very broad. The chance to employ both one's motivation as well as one's body in the process provides one with a wide selection of tools. Sharing with others who are inside this frame of wishing to benefit others brings great development, and one's knowledge of the conditioned nature and fundamental emptiness of all phenomena makes it possible to develop in all areas of life.

The fastest and most effective method to enlighten the students is through blessing i.e., sharing his absolute view, this is then called the Diamond Way. In this function, here as an accomplisher or yogi, the teacher has a great deal of power and responsibility. Unfortunately, as numerous scandals have shown, a lack of general knowledge concerning the multidimensional relationship between teacher and student make the previous warnings and a more detailed description important.

Enthusiasm was always the best raw material for quick human development. Only this feeling supplies enough power for major breakthroughs on one's way. Therefore, the highest Diamond Way and Great Seal teachings, which point out mind's essence directly, require that the chemistry between a teacher and a student fit and that the latter be deeply inspired. Until a steady state of bliss and certainty has been established and ups and downs no longer play a significant part on one's way, devotion will remain the strongest push for one's spiritual growth. After that, it will be gratitude and responsibility.

As deep feelings may easily lead to dependency, both teachers and students must know clearly what they can handle and of course be mentally fit. In essence, devotion means being open to the example that one's teacher chooses to give. A classic example is the great accomplisher Milarepa, who underwent some extremely hard times but never lost confidence in his teacher Marpa, nine hundred years ago in Tibet. His transmission is carried on by the Karma Kagyu lamas, headed today by the 17th Karmapa, Thaye Dorje; and it builds on the ability to enter into the teacher's energy field and bring it into one's life.

As most students would rather see their own expectations than the actual lama in front of them, the latter must take responsibility from the moment he agrees to teach them. If few come, he may work with them gradually and one by one. When many appear, which is the usual scenario today, a modern spiritual teacher should use the openness of the first encounter. Neither during lectures nor in his private expression should he hide his attitude towards character issues like love or politics. This permits his students to quickly ascertain if they are learning in the right place or not.

If the lama decides that there is a good basis for a working relationship and the students confirm this by attentively staying around, then an all-encompassing process commences. It will only sometimes be blissful but usually interesting, and to a large extent it unfolds via the groups that carry the teacher's activity. It finishes when a point of beyond-personal certainty has been reached; and as all start their development with preconceived ideas, periods of disillusionment are unavoidable.

From the outset ignorance and unclear spirituality are the

major obstacles. People must discriminate between what is and what is not Buddhism. Otherwise they will become ever more confused and waste precious time. One must also ensure that people do not run away from their defeats or unresolved challenges into the realm of all-accepting sweet occultism. Especially on the Diamond Way, if the lama does not make his students independent quickly and safeguard the development of all by ensuring that only healthy people join, he will soon be the shepherd to a flock of sheep. After a while, these students will become too soft to function properly in the outer world and may have at the same time become too entrenched to find a more fitting teacher. This produces a frustrated feeling in many organizations and effectively scares off the very people for whom Buddha taught the Diamond Way.

During this long process, the student's main job is to be honest with himself. After all, it concerns his development. Without expectation, fear, or unacknowledged wishes he should ask certain basic questions when first meeting a teacher: "Do I really trust him? Is he honest or just politically correct? Would I want to be like him in fifteen years?" Or, on a very practical level: "Would he stand by me in a scuffle?" or "Would I buy a used car from him?" Among men, the relationship often functions on such practical levels, while women are usually guided more through their feeling for the teacher's radiance and everyday behavior, imagining how he would be as a lover or a father. As one will gradually absorb one's teacher's tendencies and qualities, both men and women should insist that their chosen teacher, the mirror to their mind, manifests the absolute accomplishments of fearlessness, spontaneous joy, and farsighted compassion. If these factors are missing, the lama is not a reliable refuge; and his experience of mind's nature is incomplete. However satisfying a deep intellectual knowledge of Buddha's teaching may be, only those who realize mind on the level of experience—and retain its freshness and bliss in the marrow of their bones—can fully convince others through their example. Other teachers can become so-called "spiritual friends" and may also be very useful in that function.

The **"essential instructions"** mentioned next in the verse are the instructions on mind, the timeless source and experiencer of all things. The term only concerns explanations which go beyond any illusion of a separate "self" and dissolve all dualistic concepts like God and soul, Atman and Brahman, self and other. Only what points directly to the unity of experiencer, experience, and act of experiencing is liberating and enlightening. Gods and devils, pleasure and pain, are conditioned pictures in the mirror of consciousness. They appear there, change, are experienced through it, and also dissolve there once again. Only timeless mind that is in essence space, clarity, and free play in experience and without any limit in its compassionate expression is lasting. That which looks through beings' eyes and listens through their ears is timeless and true. The clear light that is conscious of all things and makes them possible is the only absolute reality. Thus Buddha's highest view of the Great Seal contains the basis, way, and goal of all enlightenment and proves mind's direct experience to be inherent power and joy. Except for the verses that supply the frame at the beginning and end of this book, as well as verse 16, Karmapa's wishes remain within the absolute view.

And finally what are those **"hindrances"** that may stop beings' development? There exist outer, inner and secret ones and they are all dangerous (see verse 24). They may darken one's consciousness during several future lives or shunt one onto a spiritual sidetrack. On the outer level, the obstacle would be losing the eighteen conditions that make conscious development possible. (They are explained traditionally in Gampopa's *The Jewel Ornament of Liberation*,[2] an important book containing Buddha's Great Way, as well as in my book on the Diamond Way Foundational Practices, *Ngondro*.[3] On the inner level it would be the loss of one's motivation to reach enlightenment for the benefit of all beings; and on the secret and most essential level, it means losing one's pure view. It expresses itself as disturbances in one's Diamond Way bond to one's lama. If this appears, the teacher must do his utmost to share his joy and turn the situation around. If the student is unable to absorb this, he should downgrade the relationship to that of shared idealism and let whoever is affected leave with his blessing and best wishes.

2. Gampopa, *The Jewel Ornament of Liberation*. (Ithaca, NY: Snow Lion Publications, 1989).
3. Lama Ole Nydahl, *Ngondro* (Nevada City, CA: Blue Dolphin, 1999).

Nagarjuna

ལུང་རིགས་ཆོས་པས་མི་ཤེས་སྒྲིབ་ལས་གྲོལ། །

Absorbing Buddha's teachings and their logic frees one from
the veil of non-comprehension.

མན་ངག་བསམ་པས་ཐེ་ཚོམ་མུན་ནག་བཅོམ། །

Examining these essential instructions conquers the darkness of
doubt.

སྒོམ་བྱུང་འོད་ཀྱིས་གནས་ལུགས་ཇི་བཞིན་གསལ། །

Through the light produced by meditation, the essence of
phenomena is recognized, the way it is.

ཤེས་རབ་གསུམ་གྱི་སྣང་བ་རྒྱས་པར་ཤོག །

May the radiance of these three wisdoms increase.

VERSE 5

The presentation of **"absorbing, examining, and meditating"** being wisdoms is unusual to Westerners. However, if one understands human development as the unfolding of a totality, this view contains another kind of logic and contributes an alternative but balanced view. As it combines thought, feeling, and experience, it has the potential to activate further levels of consciousness. Actually this comprehensive interpretation supplies the space for growth and rounds out several levels of experience. Exclusively conceptual systems, on the other hand, easily smother mind's original freshness. As Buddha's teachings are comparable to a pie that tastes good whichever way one cuts it, works like this text allow continually new approaches to a content that may bring forth inexhaustible new insights.

But let us return to the three wisdoms. What is needed for mind's full development? First, there must be sufficient and correct information; and every engaged teacher would surely envy Buddha's teaching environment. The situation he enjoyed 2,550 years ago for passing on his power was truly unique. First, among the founders of the religions known today, he had plenty of time. He taught from his enlightenment at the age of thirty-five until he died peacefully at age eighty. Second—and this condition was unknown in the West between ancient Greece, the Renaissance, and our 1960s—a large number of idealistic, intelligent, educated, and independent students were able to seek him out. Many stayed close to him and constantly wanted to know more.

He could therefore pass on the 84,000 instructions that are known today as Buddhism and have been collected in the 108 inch-thick volumes called the *Kanjur*. This sounds like a frightening amount of material, but it is all common sense. It points to mind's absolute essence and shows how to realize it. A meaningful involvement with its contents calls neither for reading glasses of increased strength nor for medications against book dust allergy. One only needs a few glasses of the ocean of Buddha's wisdom at any one time. It is of course easiest when there is a lama with life experience or a Diamond Way group nearby that can guide the enlightening meditations and teach the view. But when the readers have the right seeds in their subconscious from former lives, even a simple but clear overview of Buddha's teaching can trigger massive development.

With the growing awareness of one's present situation and a ripening understanding of the true importance of the ways and the goals, one will naturally wish to develop for the benefit of others. Such an approach contains an on-going warning against wasting time and motivates one to avoid confusion whenever possible. In addition, it permits beings to decide the primary areas they want to develop. Buddha taught "the way things are" for no other reason than to benefit beings. As enlightenment is the opening up of all capacities, including clear thought and logic, all questions must be answerable. Insistence upon convincing explanations increases their comprehensiveness and makes them more useful to people. It is a special and luminous joy when life increases in intensity and dark areas of non-comprehension dissolve. Here the West must not imitate the mistaken "good" behavior of traditional Asians. Even though the teacher may goad them, very few Chinese Buddhists ever ask questions at a lecture. Some may think that it is impolite to do this to the lama, but others probably fear a loss of face in front of others by showing that some point was not fully understood. Many, however, simply will not subject their deepest thought patterns to analysis and therefore prefer instead to consume the dharma. They may pay a great deal of money for a series of blessings and initiations for long life or wealth—or they may support a monastery instead of meditating and changing their own lives or bringing Buddhism to the man on the street.

The conveyance of Buddhist teaching belongs to the realm of the "outer" teacher. Later the "inner" teacher becomes active, where one processes the information received. "Examining," the second wisdom, is the ongoing absorption of what was learned. By testing the teachings in the world, understanding becomes certainty. As one's view widens, the flow of outer and inner events as well as the mutual interdependence of all phenomena becomes ever more apparent. Gradually both way and goal are seen on a completely practical level, and one can include relevant aspects of Buddha's teaching in each situation. One's readiness to not block out painful teachings concerning one's own situation, such as those of cause and effect, means that doubts will fall away in droves. From this point on, life only becomes more meaningful.

Wisdom's full slide from head to heart brings about the third kind of wisdom: "meditation." This is the "secret" teacher. Here the steamroller of immediate and total experience starts moving. Mind's timeless radiance shines ever more convincingly as a flow of constant, self-arisen "a-ha" experiences through whatever may appear. As soon as one has adopted the view of the Great Seal—that experiencer, experience and object experienced are in essence inseparably one—liberation and enlightenment are only a question of courage and perseverance. This explains Karmapa's last line because without well-tested knowledge, a good understanding, and self-arisen insight, one will waste masses of time.

རྟག་ཆད་མཐའ་བྲལ་བདེན་གཉིས་གཞི་ཡི་དོན།

The nature of the ground is the dual truth, free of the extreme
views of a permanent reality and of nihilism.

སྒྲོ་སྐུར་མཐའ་བྲལ་ཚོགས་གཉིས་ལམ་མཆོག་གིར

The excellent way consists of the two accumulations, free of the
restraining habits of mistaken affirmation or denial.

ཞྱིད་ཞིའི་མཐའ་བྲལ་དོན་གཉིས་འབྲས་ཐོབ་པའི།

In this way the fruit of dual benefits is reached, free of the
extremes of both conditioned existence and inert peace.

གོལ་འཁྲུག་མེད་པའི་ཚེས་དང་ཕྱད་པར་ཤོག

May we meet with this faultless teaching.

VERSE 6

Like several times later in this text, Karmapa uses a catchword to hold a series of insights together. Through its repetition he fastens his main thought in the reader's mind. Here, **"dual"** is chosen to connect between an ordinary and enlightened perception.

Buddha's teaching on dual truth cuts through the philosophical knots of countless thinkers and cultures with a masterly stroke. By pointing to apparent opposites while at the same time sharing the insights that dissolve them, he satisfies the age-old questions of eloquent rationalists and nihilists. In the first line Karmapa points to the basis of experience, the world of appearance. He describes how outer and inner phenomena are conditioned, composite, and without any nature of their own. And then he refers to the experience of unenlightened beings, who feel the world to be solid, lasting, and real.

Whoever in former lives dealt with the emptiness and dependent conditionality of all phenomena or substantially benefited others is today in an easy position. When the mirror of one's mind has only a few areas that need cleaning, the world of experiences remains dream-like; and suffering simply passes one by or is seen as being of little relevance. In each new body, however, the inner energy channels must be activated once again because this is the only all-round way to re-establish the awareness of the non-reality of appearances that was the source of the freedom one enjoyed during former lives.

As these teachings are in conflict with the world that beings know from their sensory input, the logic of these essential Buddhist teachings must break the barriers of sensual experience and habitual thought. In particular the completion phase of Diamond Way meditations deeply changes one's perceptions, melting together with the transparent buddha forms till only naked awareness remains, bringing convincing states of confidence and gratitude. These feelings then lose all limits when it is recognized that joy has no other cause than space. As can also be seen during the free fall when parachuting, even hardboiled materialists with good Karma experience a profound increase in the meaning of life. All it takes is to make that first step on this liberating way and trust space to be their friend.

All Buddhist methods aim at this total experience of awareness and phenomena, which lies beyond concepts. They remove the roots of expectations and fear, making one centered and strong. The importance of such a teaching cannot be overestimated as it is people's values that steer the world. Still today, neither the views of eternalism nor nihilism have ever managed to satisfy their advocates. If during some point in history a culture decided to see everything as real, it at first brought about a great deal of expansion and many direct experiences. This view, however, also made suffering more real, as the facts of old age, sickness, and death were still inescapable. In some more educated situations where the opposite view was chosen, stating that nothing has any reality, then every experience appeared gray. One was then without any joyful tools to handle the outer and inner worlds, while suffering was still present. Karmapa doesn't mention here any other possibilities—like existentialism (the idea that things are there because they are experienced), which can be refuted by recognizing that everything constantly changes, or transcendentalism (the idea that things have some true, mental cause elsewhere), which cannot in itself be proven. No matter what situation one is in, unless one realizes that everything is mind, it is like being lost in a foreign country without a map. No philosophy that limits the totality of existence could ever sufficiently explain the nature of all phenomena. As Gampopa said nine hundred years ago: "People who think things are real are as stupid as cows. People who think things are not real are even more stupid."

Today many scientists marvel at Buddha's profound comprehension of the nature of the material world. The same insights into the functioning of the universe seemingly occur whether one recognizes mind in meditation or examines its expressions through quantum mechanics, telescopes, or particle accelerators. These mutual confirmations are very popular and touch many who feel that things are drifting too far apart or are too lazy to investigate the details. Shakespeare's, "To be or not to be" would now more fittingly be, " To be AND not to be." Whether mind is seen as a neutral element, the potential for events, "no thing" or space charged with possibilities—experiencing the dream-like nature of everything outer and inner immediately dissolves the contradiction between the views of existence and non-existence. Everything outer or inner then appears from the potential of space, unfolds as its rich play, is recognized by its radiant awareness, and returns back into its unlimited emptiness. Not possessing any independent nature of their own, worlds, beings, and experiences appear from the meeting of countless conditions and disappear again when they disperse.

Buddha's advice for solving such contradictions, the subject of verse 9, is to recognize that the world perceived through one's senses and concepts is simply a series of frozen thought-forms that have arisen from the conditioned experiences of countless beings. If one has the good fortune to be able to improve the impressions in one's mind through an understanding of causality while removing any bad imprints, then this has the deepest of meanings. Therefore everything is achieved and enriched, and one develops a taste of freedom. Here conditioned and ultimate influences work together in life. Their good efforts help beings wake-up into liberation and ultimately enlightenment, while bad actions produce additional tightness in their lives.

The **"two accumulations"** are kind of a new concept in the West but function as the practical spine of Buddha's teaching. Not without reason, Karmapa calls it the **"excellent way."** This approach is required at each level of Buddha's teachings, and its common sense gives one a secure feeling of being in control. Building up positive impressions while removing disturbing feelings, self-centeredness and boredom, they bring inner peace, richness, and timeless bliss. Although the teachings include a basis of avoidance (the monk's vows of the Theravada), teach one how to work one's way through levels of compassion and wisdom in a balanced way (bodhisattva-work or Mahayana), and reach the final state of identification and enlightened feedback (Diamond Way), each of these stages works with these two accumulations using increasingly sophisticated methods. As they are so all-important, they will here be accessed from several sides.

If limiting one's exposure to life's possible pain is compared to walking, developing a rich inner life is analogous to driving a car while utilizing the Great Seal teachings on mind; the buddha forms, mantras, and breathing techniques are like learning to fly. As mind was always enlightened in its essence, each step employs the above two repetitive processes for its realization, which perfect one another. They are the accumulation of positive impressions in mind, which makes it relax, and the development of the resulting inherent wisdom.

One may compare the first step of conscious good deeds with the sun's path to zenith, while wisdom is like removing the clouds. When both have been achieved, all things are clearly seen. Another much used metaphor is that of ascending a staircase. One does or says something useful and mind finds peace. From this relaxation, self-arisen states of insight appear—the "a-ha" experiences. They verify that an action is right and in keeping with the wishes of beings. Accordingly one will do more positive actions and receive further insights until mind experiences beauty and meaning on every level. Deeply confident because of this, like a sky-diver one takes a leap beyond the fixed realm of concepts into awareness itself and thus shares the liberation of all who manifest this trust. Although the ecstatic awareness of mind's radiance can only be held after many years, from the first experience of the clear light, which one's lama's blessing made possible, one recognizes it as one's essence. One thus continues practicing with a greater involvement and produces more positive imprints that lead to further wisdom.

As nothing can add further perfection to everybody's inherent buddha nature, the teachings only help mind's timeless abilities manifest. Thus one learns to see things as they are. One does not need to ascribe further qualities or deny what is there. While they unfold, many events are recognized to be deeply familiar and a great gift. Mind better understands that something basically good is happening and feels confidence. One experiences a self-liberating wisdom that perfects situations much more effectively, clearly, and comprehensively than anything conceptual. The position of one's ego is seriously undermined when insecurity and awkward conduct falls away. When it finally deflates due to a lack of sustenance, there is nothing to prove or excuse anymore; and no obstacle can hinder one's own happiness or block one's work for others. One will then do what is relevant; and as others always vastly outnumber oneself, they will usually take first priority. Thus the **"dual benefit"** appears. In Buddhism suffering simply means that one has made mistakes. With this insight—that everything is beyond-personal—it is possible to live without needing to play the role of a victim. In the long run, everyone benefits from any one individual's development because of the all-pervading and composite nature of all things. This is because in its true and timeless essence, all is freedom, richness, and fun. The great reward of the yogic accomplisher is the gift of increasingly recognizing the suchness of both mind and phenomena. Therefore being able to really help others becomes something so intrinsically right that any contact with this sort of activity brings joy. Everybody has benefit through this view.

After the basis and way described in the former lines, Karmapa here mentions the **"fruit."** Its first and fleeting appearances show one just how many levels of disturbance have already been removed. **"Conditioned existence"** is what was called *samsara* in Sanskrit and **"inert peace"** is the small nirvana. These concepts are often explained in great detail, but this is not necessary for the keen observer. As most beings are clearly caught in such states, one has only to watch the world to see what they entail.

Conditioned existence or confusion arises because unenlightened mind works like an eye; it sees only the outer world and not itself. As the experiencer does not recognize itself behind the experiences, one then has no center, charges after one's passing impressions, assumes subjective experience to be real, and in the end suffers because everything is impermanent. It produces life's vast cattle market where everyone is searching for something but nobody is ultimately satisfied. Birth, old age, sickness, loss, and death are the most classic concerns of humans; but they also try to get what they want, avoid what they do not like, hold onto what they have, and make do with whatever they cannot avoid.

The **"inert peace"** is also unbalanced. It is a state of avoidance, of not wanting to face or experience what is there. Here one sits in a homemade bunker surrounded by barbed wire, without any outside contact. By not knowing what is going on, one succeeds in avoiding much of life's suffering. One is, however, of little use to others and can barely develop beyond a certain level. This realization is known as the small nirvana or personal liberation, the cessation of disturbing emotions and the state of an Arhat. Over more than two thousand years of debate, the southern schools of Buddhism defined this as the highest level that may be obtained until a new Buddha manifests.

In the northern schools, full enlightenment is accomplished through the additional removal of all stiff ideas. It is called the "great nirvana," the abolition of ignorance, full enlightenment, and buddhahood. This level contains and transcends both the conditioned world and the state of peace. Western accomplishers might call it the "non-sticky nirvana," because mind equally celebrates whatever happens and does not happen.

And finally, why does Karmapa proclaim Buddha's teaching to be faultless? Because it brings the result. Containing both way and goal, it brings liberation and enlightenment and thus produces timeless bliss. Striving towards this goal is an obvious choice. And there is no alternative.

སྦྱང་གཞི་ སེམས་ཉིད་ གསལ་ སྟོང་ ཟུང་ འཇུག་ ལ།

The basis of purification is mind itself, its union of clarity, and emptiness.

སྦྱོང་ བྱེད་ ཕྱག་ ཆེན་ རྡོ་ རྗེ་ རྣལ་ འབྱོར་ ཆེ །

The method of purification is the Great Seal, the diamond-like practice.

སྦྱང་ བྱ་ གློ་ བུར་ འཁྲུལ་ པའི་ དྲི་ མ་ རྣམས །

The object of purification is the fleeting illusory impurities.

སྦྱངས་ འབྲས་ དྲི་ བྲལ་ ཆོས་ སྐུ་ མངོན་ གྱུར་ ཤོག །

May we accomplish the fruit of purification, the perfectly pure state of truth.

VERSE 7

The concept of purification holds this new verse together, which once again is teeming with profound meaning. Its subject matter encompasses the basis of perfection, the means to accomplish it and finally the fruit—enlightenment itself. Under the heading of buddha nature or way and goal, it exemplifies the ultimate freedom of all beings. As mind is in its essence enlightenment and one with whatever appears in time and space, everything can be realized. With the necessary drive, timeless liberation and enlightenment can be reached. Although experiences are limitless in their expression, like images and waves, the mirror and the ocean remain unchanged. Therefore, Tibetans compare truth to the reflection of a moon. Wherever there is a puddle, it is seen. As mind is always empty and radiant, one can ultimately rely on the experiencer of phenomena; space cannot be harmed by anything. This joyful realization is recognized in the first line of this verse.

The way a surfer lets a funny little wave pass by, knowing that a better one will soon follow, Karmapa advises his readers to look beyond all changing and unclear experiences and trust that mind's timeless essence is naturally rich. As the experiencer is in essence space and thus perfect and indestructible, everything is mind's gift to itself. Therefore there is no reason to make dramas about the clarity of this space. Whatever manifests, pleasant or unpleasant, is nothing but mind's outer and inner play.

In Western cultures, this view has an intensely liberating effect. It releases one from a misperception that was adopted from Hinduism during the sixties, the idea that thoughts harm one's meditation. It also helps Christians who find themselves unable to have only good thoughts. However unceasing or sinful the surfacing impressions may appear, being nothing but mind no impurity is possible inside or out. Everything arises from its luminous space, changes in it, is experienced through it, and returns to that same radiant awareness. Whoever is used to the principle of purity in belief-religions can take a sigh of relief at this point. Buddha had no fear of the body. He did not wish spiritual solutions upon the world that would suppress any part of a being's life. They would be unnatural and need to be constantly protected. Instead, he advises a powerful kind of purity that consciously feeds on life's countless mixed events and thus gathers unshakable wisdom for the good of all. No virgin, sheltered from life, could symbolize this state—but rather a well-loved, mature woman whose wise gaze, fed by experience, penetrates the world.

Thus in its essence mind is empty, no thing; but at the same time it is rich in nature, clear, and conscious. If it were not basically pure, then how could one clean it? Washing a piece of coal would simply make it smaller. However, the same process applied to a diamond makes it shine ever more. Like an effective detergent, the Foundational Practices and other Diamond Way methods will also discolor the wash water for a while. Then however, it will show clearly that mind's final state is indestructible and radiant, like this king of stones.

The Great Seal develops the certainty that space, manifestation, and perception are interdependent, inseparably one, and expressions of the same mind. Whoever fully processes this will dwell blissfully in both the ocean and its waves. Thus one will also recognize that, on the relative level of likes and dislikes, every impression returns back into space and is thereby purified. Because its space and clarity are both basically pure, mind only needs to recognize this.

Although, so far, few have managed to fully conquer their disturbing feelings, the opponent is not an eight hundred pound gorilla in the opposite corner of the ring. One only needs to understand how the feelings function and can then choose to either let them tie themselves into knots or direct their energy towards a chosen purpose. There is no reason to feel moralistic about disturbing feelings. They do not spring from an absolute evil—which in itself is an impossibility, since it would self-destruct from all the negative feedback it would receive. Instead, their cause is mind's beginningless inability to recognize its all-embracing potential. That it is subject, object, and action all at once. This brings about the main and secondary disturbing feelings that, again, produce clumsy actions and hurtful words. When their effects ripen, the beings involved suffer and feel captive. And worst of all, if unrecognized and left untreated, the habits that arise will only lead one to activities that result in further pain.

Although they have always governed the world of unenlightened beings, all disturbed kinds of consciousness remain superficial. They cannot influence mind's ultimate state. Buddha's compassionate insight here truly helps those who have been conditioned to feel tortured by remorse and guilt. He asks: How can something be ultimately sinful or dirty when it arises from the purity of space, plays in its openness, is known through its clarity, and disappears back into its potentiality?

A growing recognition that disturbing feelings are just hot air or meaningless drama makes harmful behavior less and less compulsive. Even Khomeni, Pol Pot, Hitler, Stalin, and

Mao had buddha nature. Their sick inner states of mind and criminal outer actions happened in the radiant space, which they share with everything, were registered by the same fundamental intelligence, and are now being re-experienced in their full horror by those gentlemen, thanks to mind's unlimited potential. What marks them apart from healthy beings is that they had no distance from their hate. The collective suffering that occurred was also triggered by the bad karma of the people, who played along in one role or another, because of their own ignorance and disturbing feelings.

All who recognize that conditioned feelings were not there before, will soon be gone, and are right now changing all the time, are on their way to getting the upper hand. The Diamond Way and Great Seal teachings then provide almost limitless methods for putting such disturbed energies to good use. In fact, as the strongest ones provide the biggest push forward, there is never any lack of excitement.

Illusions that simply express mind's confused movements can thus be gradually converted into wisdom and activity. As the purpose of any spiritual path should be mind's recognition of itself for the benefit of all, it is most important that one's powerful but untrained consciousness can here learn to know itself.

On the highest level, a non-judgmental attitude is key, so that disturbing thoughts and feelings can be purified by being trivialized. If one simply lets them tag along despite whatever else is happening, while giving them no attention, they will soon run out of steam. However, one should not miss out on the chance to have a good laugh at what is being presented. Sometimes it is as dramatic as a good thriller at the cinema, and one may choose to gather insights whenever something unusual is offered. Seen from this angle, one's mixed selection of changing feelings will show one how to benefit others later. While shaking one's head with incredulity that one could ever have taken them seriously, these internal tigers become visibly thinner and the crocodiles lose their teeth. Disturbing feelings live from the affirmation they receive. If denied, they gradually lose their power.

The realization that pain and other difficulties only have the power that one gives them liberates one from the mental veils, which in essence are always changing and superficial. Enough space is then freed up, in order to experience the joyful certainty that fearless wisdom, self-arisen joy and active love are mind's true nature. No more enticing track to enlightenment can exist.

གཞི་ལ་སྒྲོ་འདོགས་ཆོད་པ་ལྟ་བའི་གདེངས།

Conviction of view results from cutting out doubts concerning the ground.

དེ་ལ་མ་ཡེངས་སྐྱོང་བབསྐྱམ་པའི་གནད།

The crux of one's meditation is holding this view without distraction.

སྐོམ་དོན་ཀུན་ལ་རྩལ་སྦྱང་སྦྱད་པའི་མཆོག

Excellent action consists of mastering all meditations.

ལྟ་སྐོམ་སྦྱད་པའི་གདེངས་དང་ལྡན་པར་ཤོག

May we obtain certainty of view, meditation, and action.

VERSE 8

.

The goal of Buddha's teaching is experience—that beings recognize the nature of things. He is only interested in spiritual growth and knows no half measures. Over the past 2,500 years numerous scientific breakthroughs have shown more and more of his statements to be true. However, if at some stage science were to prove some point to be wrong, Buddha himself would advise his students to trust science, at least for the time being and on the relative level. Not wishing to establish dogmas, he wants his teachings to be logically convincing and relevant to life. Detailed enquiry is invited, although it usually discloses that the questioner lacks information or is trying to twist formal statements that Buddha and his lamas try to avoid giving.

If we have managed to connect with authentic Buddhist sources, the need for a teacher grows progressively with the depth of the teaching. In the Diamond Way, he is essential because he gives blessing, methods, and power and is needed to cut through any confusion as to the way and the goal. The former concerns how things appear on the relative level and the latter how they actually are in essence, our absolute understanding. Even well-educated Westerners lose out on the fun here. They are not used to relaxed transparency and clarity within a religion. For that reason they don't expect this and only gradually allow themselves the freedom of not being bound by dogmas and the need to believe. Then, however, they jump with joy at the chance to employ intellect, experience, and emotional capacities in their development.

Buddha's teachings can thus only benefit from a profound examination. As I mentioned in verse 4, it is even possible to doubt one's entire way up to liberation—although this procedure is slow and may fail to bring one to a flying finish. Buddha's confidence in his students is shown clearly in the freedom he gives them to trust their own minds. He does not force them to make automatic moralistic judgments, which so often completely miss the point. This is particularly true when it concerns the liberating and sometimes controversial activities of the bodhisattvas. They are the people who free others. Having understood the dream-like nature of all existence, they can help beings to mature in effective but unconventional ways.

Instead, Buddha wishes that his students should allow themselves the luxury of a gray zone whenever possible. This means a field of awareness where pieces of information, which do not need to be acted upon decisively or at once, can mature. Here one's store of knowledge can stay abreast of new developments, and insights may accrue naturally while one makes the best of all situations. The mature, good feeling spread by people who are able to speak and act from an intelligent conviction, without political correctness or brainwashing, is like a relaxing balm for the confused world of today. Actually, nothing has brought more suffering and suppression to people than the attempts of religions or absolutist world views (like communism and fascism) to force their followers into immediate action in unclear situations. This tendency is the root of countless human tragedies on both individual and collective levels. Among the starters of major religions, Buddha apparently stands alone in his fundamental trust in beings; and that is a pity. Nothing is more beautiful than free people.

Therefore, Buddha always invited questions whenever he was teaching and never applied any pressure on people to believe. One should only accept what one is convinced about, since any true development will only take place on the basis of understanding and confidence. Buddha wanted neither sheep nor "yes-men," but rather colleagues. With ever less distraction, whoever is inspired by his teachings and uses them in meditation will first meet with and then be able to hold the experience of their innate buddha nature. Thus, insight deepens the Great Seal teachings into all-pervading experience, and whatever doubts may surface on the way are transformed into understanding. Merely remaining in a state of naked awareness dissolves any knot in one's mind. Most convincingly, anger turns into clear and undisturbed perception. Receding pride lets one notice the multi-faceted nature and richness of existence. Dissolving attachment teaches us the skill of discrimination. Jealousy disappears in the sequence of experiences. Finally, where ignorance and confusion once clouded our view, ever more frequent and joyful moments of intuitive insight take their place.

Thus, the Diamond Way meditations connect mind with its timeless essence. Beyond hope and fear, clinging and aversion, they bring it to absolute certainty. The way a cup of coffee settles and then reflects, the hooks of enlightening teachings catch the rings of beings' innate wisdom. Thus mind's power of awareness appears ever more frequently between and behind the experiences, and in the very moment of actuality it manifests as timeless clear light.

Once again, Buddha's Great Seal teachings are unique and provide the ultimate level of view. Instead of trying to avoid thoughts (which brings about the dreaded white wall effect) or clinging to pleasant experiences (which nobody has yet succeeded in maintaining), Karmapa advises building real solidity through resting in the state of being conscious. This absolute confidence in the experiencer itself is a unique sign of Buddha's teaching and has since been passed on by several so far unbroken lineages of accomplishers. When Milarepa's students were irritated by thoughts or feelings, he often answered, "How can you be disturbed by bushes and waves when you know the vastness of the mountains and the boundlessness of oceans?" Other Great Seal teachings compare thoughts to thorns and mind with an elephant. The thorns may sting but elephants have very thick skins. Whoever rests consciously in whatever was understood and recognized to be true, really meditates. As mind is thus purified and gains in strength, one simply becomes a better person.

In many non-Buddhist environments, and some Buddhist ones as well, meditation has today become a collective term for practices that mainly bring about strong experiences. Hyperventilation through erratic breathing, the excited yelling of certain syllables, the pressing of the ears and eyes, long periods of mere sitting without adequate instruction, naked walks in the woods, re-birthing and spiritual palmistry are just some of the teachings offered. All traditional Buddhist meditations, on the other hand, have only one goal: to enable the practitioner to remain effortlessly in what is. This does not entail any "spiritual" contemplation, however, which often makes people exotic and confused. It is also neither a forced avoidance of thoughts that dulls mind nor an attempt to hold on to conditioned pleasant states, which is simply not possible. The only target for mind is to know itself and thus its full potential. The experience of its liberated qualities is an intense experience of joy that is as constant as its source, mind's free play. Here, all richness manifests effortlessly and actions springing from such inner surplus convince both others and oneself.

This is precisely the meaning of **"excellent action"**— scooping from the abundance of space with the certainty that highest truth is highest bliss and that space is in essence boundless. This fresh courage, liberating all, unfolds through polishing the jewel of the mind. Thus whatever was recognized as relevant is absorbed into one's heart center. To the holder of the experience, it is a state of natural abiding and centeredness under all conditions. Friends notice a quality of self-arisen joy, and one feels enriched through one's balanced expression of compassion and beyond-personal understanding. In daily life these qualities manifest as an inspired and useful lifestyle that pleases many. Thus there is only increasing gain as the practical but narrow view of "either-or" is placed in the liberating context and the wide-reaching frame of "both-and."

Whoever is able to keep his bonds—especially to his first Diamond Way teacher—will gradually perfect his methods and qualities, the greatest of gifts. While the enlightened powerfields around the students mature in tandem with those inside their bodies, there will be no limit to their growth.

Meditation, all in all, means not losing awareness of consciousness itself. Many feel the great importance of this point, but few manage to hold on to it. Admittedly it is not easy, and the speed of one's progress depends to a high degree on the practice done during former lives. Much effort is required to keep this view until the experience of what is being conscious—of that which is all around, behind everything, and knows all events—solidifies. When life situations remain open and dream-like and the space for free choice is experienced everywhere, the roots of negative feeling are cut. Ignorance, however, was there since beginningless time and the fight against such a tenacious enemy is not easily won.

Every ounce of effort is meaningful, as there is a long road ahead. Whoever manages to find twenty to thirty minutes— or more—every day for the highly effective Diamond Way meditations will do well. By uniting with our lama, possibly in the form of one of the buddha forms (yidams) of energy and light, there will be certain growth—if we don't happen to also work as a butcher or sell drugs to minors. Each mantra is meaningful; each new contact with the Great Seal brings results. When view, meditation, and action complement each other in life, the perfections that were wished for materialize. With intense delight, we witness the most important trans-formations. Here, impressions that were planted in beings' store-consciousness since beginningless time self-liberate into wisdoms; and it becomes natural to support a Diamond Way center with one's friends for the benefit of many.

Shavaripa

ཆོས་རྣམས་ཐམས་ཅད་སེམས་ཀྱི་རྣམ་འཕྲུལ་ཏེ།

All phenomena are manifestations of mind.

སེམས་ནི་སེམས་མེད་སེམས་ཀྱི་ངོ་བོས་སྟོང་།

Mind is not "a" mind; it is empty in essence.

སྟོང་ཞིང་མ་འགགས་ཆིར་ཡང་རུང་བ་སྟེ།

Although empty, all things arise in every way without hindrance.

ལེགས་པར་བརྟག་ནས་གཞི་རུ་ཆོད་པར་ཤོག།

May precise observation sever mistaken views about the ground.

Verse 9

"All phenomena are manifestations of mind."

Everything outer and inner is mind's free play. This understanding, that beings' perception of the world is dependent
upon their inner state, enjoys a rising popularity today in the
educated West. This recognition usually comes quite easily
when it concerns others, but people are often not so convinced when in the grasp of their own mental gymnastics.
Most will agree, however, that somehow one meets nice people when one is in a good mood, while if one is on a bad trip,
miserable characters and faults appear everywhere. As heaven
and hell therefore so evidently happens in mind, beings are
continuously creating their future worlds. The impressions
that one determines as significant—and are therefore seeds in
one's store consciousness—determine whether one views the
world through rose-tinted or blackened glasses. In Sanskrit
this law of cause and effect is called *karma,* in Tibetan *lae.*
Buddha teaches that such conditioned states, the play of
timeless space, have no beginning. They are also not absolute
and only retain their power until mind has recognized its
unborn nature, the indestructible mirror behind its changing
impressions.

Here Buddha's wisdom frees the certitude that highest
truth is highest bliss. It seems that other religions are rarely
aware that any unfolding of mind's power is in essence rich
and joyful. The Tibetan word for this spontaneous process is

Detong, meaning space and bliss inseparable. And this highest view liberates all.

This is the inner aspect of Karmapa's words. Their meaning goes further, however. The teaching that everything is mind also covers the outer world. Two thousand five hundred and fifty years ago, Buddha predicted some of the most important discoveries of modern science, which Karmapa here condenses. He declares the collectively experienced world to be beings' karma directing mind's free play, and that is no more lasting or real than a shared dream. Since the time of the 3rd Karmapa, light has been condensed into particles; and the separation between being and non-being, once seen as absolute, is now understood to be relative. Existence and non-existence are today explained as two aspects of the same totality. Skillfully explained, such statements remove all limitations in time and space. They show what is absolute and conditioned, where the "both-and" and "either-or" views are relevant. Thus, they remove the last concepts and lead to mind's full enlightenment.

How may the formation and dissolution of universes be explained with dualistic concepts? Here is Buddha's view:

After a world burns up—described in terms very similar to what current astronomers envisage for our planetary system in ten billion years—somewhere in space, those beings who are still not liberated and had no experience of their timeless essence join the minds of inhabitants of other formerly existent worlds. When sufficient karmic energy has accumulated, a new galaxy condenses automatically. As space is not a black hole but contains all possibilities, nothing illogical like an external creator is necessary. This whole process may be observed from pure and impure points of view, but these are not equal in value or truth. The former enlightens beings and is timelessly true while the second springs from fundamental ignorance. Thus, the insight into the composite richness of all things—the pride of unenlightened beings—causes everything solid to appear; and from the mirror-like wisdom—their anger—springs everything fluid. Discriminating wisdom—beings' attachments—manifests as the element of heat; and the wisdom of experience—their jealousy—appears as constant movement like wind. Finally basic ignorance—the cause for experiencing space as a state of separation—becomes all-pervading wisdom that carries information and surrounds one.

Ever more frequently, one then becomes certain that limitless space and countless universes lie behind beings and that the distance between them is negligible. While the outer frame or world condenses from the collective consciousness of beings, their individual karmas manifest as their experiences, bodies, environments, and tendencies. Therefore, the teaching that everything is mind is a central pillar of Buddhism. Not only are one's filtered experiences of the world mind, but the world itself is mind.

When beings have physically developed to the stage of being capable of absolute insights, then the limitless power and love inherent in space expresses itself as Buddhas who teach the ways of liberation and enlightenment. It is said that one thousand will manifest in this world while there is intelligent life and that Sakyamuni Gautama of our time was the fourth. Everything in their lives is an example; their only goal is to liberate all beings from ignorance and pain; and their influence often lasts for thousands of years. Their teachings consist of five periods of equal length. When a Buddha starts a new period where the teachings are known, people first obtain realization in a very quick and direct manner through inspiration and identification. After that, they then reach enlightenment in a slower, more rounded way through meditation. In the next phase, they have lost the total approach and work intellectually. After that again, people are satisfied with formal rituals and robes. And finally, after a time of further decay, even cause and effect are forgotten and the influence of that Buddha is over. People treat others and themselves roughly, and only after much unnecessary trouble do they again become willing to free enough space between their disturbing feelings that another Buddha can appear and teach. Through his teachings, the above sequence of spiritual opportunities arises once more, and hopefully many beings again reach liberation or enlightenment until that period of absolute view is again lost.

Applying this course of events to Buddha Sakyamuni and Asia, then the five periods, each of the five hundred years that he predicted, finished fifty years ago. It is most disturbing when unpleasant prophecies are fulfilled with accuracy, but it was precisely at this time that the traditional practice of Buddhist teachings declined dramatically in Asia.

In Japan, Thailand, and among exiled Chinese people, the cause was greed and materialism—while central and eastern continental Asia suffered from communist suppression and the killing of the educated class. The cultures of the rest of Indochina and Sri Lanka became embroiled in politics and war. Almost everywhere Buddhist traditions have become ossified and ritualized as our practices became irrelevant to the needs of a modern life. After the Muslim destruction of northern India one thousand years ago, which showed the weakness of Buddhism on the everyday level, people once again got into their ivory towers, started treating karma like fate, and forgot about educating the masses or popularizing the teachings. This sequence of events has been the cause for the destruction of many Buddhist cultures. Today, only the state of Bhutan and the Tibetan refugees of the three old Diamond Way schools preserve what is considered the whole range of Buddha's teachings. It does seem, however, that sufficient numbers of people with suitable karmas have taken rebirth in the West for the teachings to continue here. Hopefully, these essential insights into mind's essence can now massively benefit the free European cultures around the world and may one day be taken back to bless Asia, in new and engaging forms.

These comments on Karmapa's first statement—that all things are mind—were made while looking through a telescope and are generally quite a relief for people. One does not have to face the emptiness of phenomena head-on and there can at least be the expectation that mind is something. This however disappears in the following lines where the examination continues under a microscope.

Having recognized that the outer world can be reduced to the manifestation of mind and that events on the inner level are also mind's fabrication, then looking for mind is a shock, like a cold shower. The material world suddenly loses its essence. Nothing can be found. Nothing exists. Looking for mind, that also cannot be found. It has no size, color, weight, form, taste, or voltage. It is also not composed of some "subtle" material, as those with little confidence in space would like to imagine. Mind possesses no characteristic through which it can be substantiated. In essence it is empty and not a thing. The fact that consciousness is inherent in this space, which non-meditators may also suspect during moments of sudden inspiration, is mind's truth-state.

"Although empty, all things arise in every way without hindrance."

This line points to the qualities that are experienced as mind's clarity and limitless nature. It contains the levels of the joy-state and of the compassionate activity state, which expresses itself as far-sighted, useful actions. It reaches beings through those who have made the promise to take re-birth in order to help others. Though mind is without any characteristics of its own, still everything inner and outer appears as its inherent richness. Joy and useful actions spring from its space, play there freely, are recognized by its clarity, and effortlessly disappear back into its limitless essence. Although it cannot be proven to be any "thing," mind still manifests a boundless number of possibilities. It gives birth to all phenomena, lets everything happen, and encompasses and experiences whatever may occur in outer or inner space.

This verse supplies a wide-open door to unusual, enlightened states of mind and it can be analyzed from several sides. The most convincing simile for the essence of Karmapa's view would be that of a dream. The outer world of constant change is the collective dream of beings and their individual dreams, while the multitude of experiences of these processes are due to the differences in beings' stored impressions (karma), mood, genetics, previous experiences, sense impressions, and educational background.

Faults in one's perception are, however, avoidable. Beings must not stay chained to what is conditioned but have methods, an absolute goal, and the chance to develop themselves. Good dreams are the basis for waking up from the current state of ignorance into liberation and enlightenment, while the results of harmful actions bind one ever more strongly by inducing yet more suffering. This essentially unreal quality encompasses both the essence of thoughts and feelings and the supposedly solid world we experience. This is demonstrated by various experiments such as those of a group of German scientists twenty years ago. They showed that the smallest particles of an atom disappear when they collide in particle accelerators, something that materialistic philosophers were reluctant to accept for a long time. Later, their American colleagues showed that containers with perfect vacuums fill spontaneously with particles. There can thus be no absolute contradiction between being and non-being. Appearance and non-appearance can best be understood as two sides of the same totality. In a world full of prohibitions and dogmas, such insights provide a wonderful feeling of space. They show one the conditioned nature of all phenomena and thereby help one mature. The realization that only mind's unlimited, radiant space, the experiencer, is real and true while all experiences come, change and go, is totally liberating. So far nobody has managed to produce the machine that can convincingly prove that the world is formed from the mental imprints of its inhabitants, but some recent experiments in Japan once again illustrated how mind affects the inanimate world. By freezing and unfreezing samples of water, they saw that the crystal patterns formed were dependent on what the experimenter said to the samples while they were defrosted. Saying nothing left them unchanged while speaking kindly or harshly produced different results.

Karmapa's last wish, that a precise analysis of mind may reveal its essence, carries on in further verses. Avoiding drama, he shows beings how to skillfully improve the world of appearance as well as understand the absolute truth, which it has always demonstrated.

ཡོད་མ་མྱོང་བའི་རང་སྣང་ཡུལ་དུ་འཁྲུལ།

Mind's self-expression, which has never existed as such,
is mistaken for an object.

མ་རིག་དབང་གིས་རང་རིག་བདག་ཏུ་འཁྲུལ།

Due to ignorance, self-awareness is mistaken for an "I."

གཉིས་འཛིན་དབང་གིས་སྲིད་པའི་སྐྱོང་དུ་འཁྱམས།

Clinging to this duality causes one to wander within the
conditioned world.

མ་རིག་འཁྲུལ་པའི་རྩད་དང་ཆོད་པར་ཤོག།

May ignorance, the root of illusion, be cut away.

VERSE 10

The first two lines make the ears of the modern Diamond Way Buddhist pick up. In contrast to today's usual approach, Karmapa first points to mind's clarity and then to its space-nature. He presents the pictures before the mirror, mentions the waves ahead of the ocean and thus puts more weight on the experiences than the experiencer. But why does he do this? On the one hand, an unexpected angle on something may increase one's comprehension, while on the other he is probably consciously including his students with less ability for abstract thinking. Most simple people who are caught up in life feel their impermanent experiences to be very real.

"Mind's self-expression, which has never existed as such, is misunderstood as an object."

Due to basic ignorance, mind's continuous activity, which manifests outwardly as worlds and situations, is experienced as real and existent. So are the thoughts and feelings that appear inside unenlightened beings. One thinks: "This exists. This experience, this event is true." The main reason for this misinterpretation of the world is the slowness of our sense organs and the fact that our brain mainly works to exclude whatever information is not relevant to our survival. If, however, one accurately examines the outer as well as the inner world, nothing is solid. Everything vibrates, flows, and changes constantly—be it worlds, atoms, thoughts, or feelings. What is experienced as being real is actually a permanent stream of changes. First, for instance, a glass of water is seen as an outer object. When drunk, it becomes part of one; and later, after some carbon and nitrogen have been added, it may hopefully nourish some flowers. Inner conditions change in a similar way. Sometimes beings have more distance to the process and sometimes it catches them completely. Although the films change constantly, up until one's liberation one still considers this whole Disneyland to be real.

In the same way that mind's expression, its clarity, **"is misunderstood as an object"** and thus separate, its power of awareness, the experiencer, **"is misinterpreted as an 'I.'"** This duality, however, is only a concept. Old Buddhist texts use the example of air in a clay container; when broken, the separation between air inside and outside disappears although the former difference was also only illusionary. To be really existent, phenomena must show some permanence, a lasting essence; and only aware space fulfills these criteria. Empty, as it is in essence, it is free of all limiting characteristics. Unbound by time and place, it contains all perfect qualities. Being at the same time compassionately active, it offers a true refuge. The first two lines go back to verse 2 and describe the source of all suffering. As Karmapa's wishes focus on benefiting beings here and now, it is worth an in-depth look at its cause and the possible routes of escape.

Two thousand five hundred and fifty years ago, Buddha did not tire of explaining to his students how disturbances attack what is otherwise such a competent mind. He compared it to an eye that recognizes everything outside but cannot see itself. Thus experiencing the observing space, the truth-aspect of mind misunderstands itself to be an "I." Although one's body is not indestructible, and feelings and thoughts possess no recognizable qualities such as size, color, or form, because of habits that had no beginning, these faulty perceptions have embedded themselves. Mind's attachment to its changing impressions turns its clarity—all that mind experiences—into a "you" or something separate. Only enlightenment confers the power to recognize space and its intuitive wisdom, the experiencer and its objects, as aspects of mind's boundlessness. Therefore, while we are not enlightened, disturbing feelings are present. They are ignorance, egotistical desire, and ill will; and their ugly offspring are exclusive pride, greed, and envy. Buddha speaks of eighty-four thousand possible mental veils or disturbing emotions, which are all possible combinations of these six feelings. Although conditioned and always changing, they are experienced as being real and therefore bring about clumsy thoughts, words, and actions. The harmful impressions sown here mature later as difficulties on the mental and worldly levels. One then creates the causes for further difficulties by habitually blaming others and repeating one's mistakes.

If beings could see what these disturbed states really are, everything would be easy. One would recognize them as bad films playing on one's inner screen and wisely let them pass without distraction. That, however, is rarely the case. The very fact that beings are not enlightened produces their inability to choose pleasant mental states and sideline the painful ones. Instead, one believes disturbing feelings upon their arrival and usually lacks the overview that one caused these states oneself. Unaware that all beings are constantly creating their own future, one once again acts or speaks from a shortsighted motivation; and this makes it impossible to leave the wheel of conditioned existence.

"Clinging to this duality causes one to wander within the conditioned world."

Holding on to any kind of duality is characteristic of non-Buddhist points of views. One only sees what is experienced and that many different situations happen to one. Until liberation is reached, everybody is unable to recognize that only the experiencer is real and one with everything. Therefore it is probably useful to analyze this more closely here.

"Experiencing-space" and its contents such as feelings, thoughts, situations, and worlds, are felt to be separate. A deeper examination, however, shows a relationship more akin to an ocean and its waves and currents—or to water vapor, clouds, and rain. They are each expressions of the same totality. Debates concerning existence or non-existence have been held ever since man's brain became able to formulate abstract thought. Although the discoveries of the last century would have one believe that this has been a one-sided argument, a look further back in history shows that this was not always the case. The ancient Greeks, for example, felt threatened by the dream-like and ungraspable. They generally disliked the teachings about the conditioned nature and ultimate emptiness of everything that came to them from Buddhism in India. They needed something reassuringly existent and real and therefore decided to invent the concept of an *atomos*, today's atom—an idea that was quite simply plucked from thin air. The word means "indivisible" and thus gave them some conceptual reassurance, because if one could split things endlessly, then maybe finally nothing would be left and one might be facing a black hole. They also resisted the notion of the teacher as an abstract spiritual example. So, soon after their first encounter with Buddhism, the groups that had settled in India became the first to erect a statue of its founder. It must be seen as a genuine compliment that the matrix chosen was that of Apollo, the Greek god of love.[1]

Up until Karl Marx and on to what will now probably be the final departure for materialism—because of the latest

1. Stephen Batchelor, *The Awakening of the West*. (Parallax Press, Berkeley CA, 1994).

insights of modern science—different views have alternated in popularity over the last millennia concerning the reality of things; but none were truly satisfactory. Although to affirm experiences as being real leads to fleeting moments of feeling in control, it also confirms old age, sickness, death, and eventually suffering to be real. An opposing view brings even less satisfaction, as negating one's experience removes no pain. Then everything just becomes gray, the world loses its meaning, and one is left with no tools to improve the situation. Therefore, popular philosophies moved to and fro between materialistic and nihilistic standpoints until the industrial revolution gave a purpose to views supporting the former.

Up until our idealistic sixties, people's perception changed steadily towards the universe being seen as some "Great Machine"; and while becoming richer and more empowered in the outer lives, they dutifully tied up their own philosophies of life ever more tightly. The world's outer as well as beings' inner diversity were explained as being caused by coincidences and conditions and seemed to be without any absolute meaning. Meaningful concepts of existence could thus only survive in the corners of life that were not yet occupied by materialism, such as the realms of spirituality and psychology. One point subconsciously disturbed many, although few took up the challenge: By accepting the brain as the producer of consciousness, its destruction would logically entail mind's ending. This remained a sore point because it contradicted the countless observations and wishes of beings. Therefore, when parking became difficult after the war and thirty brands of toothpaste had brought no illumination, the brave and educated West needed, and was ready for, a giant step forward.

The first icebreakers were chemical and promised more than they could give. LSD showed a generation of hopefuls a door to mind's potential but took nobody through it and left many disturbed. Our blissful, beyond-dual insights into the oneness of consciousness and the world, however, have later been proved through science. As increasingly accurate instruments examine both the smallest particles and the cosmos, still no experiments seem to detract from recognizing the ultimate essence of everything material to be space.

Looking also inwardly, the experiencer that knows and understands may convincingly be understood to be conscious space, while beings' mental experiences are its free play, like streams moving in the ocean. These have been held together since beginningless time by the illusion of a "self"; and it is therefore difficult to avoid the mixed experiences of an unenlightened mind. Not realizing the experiencer to be absolute and timeless, it finds no way to transcend causality and therefore reacts to the loss of each body by searching for another conditioned situation. It could actually all be so easy! Mind never had any limiting characteristics. It was always indestructible like space and without beginning or end. Until this fact is recognized, however, it will experience the stream of its impressions as true and use body and speech to produce further **"causes for one to continue to wander within the conditioned world."**

As previously mentioned, this transient dream-like nature does not only apply to inner events but also to the outer world. This collectively experienced outer dream therefore also has no real existence. The particles of which it consists continually shift and return to the potential from which they arose. Unfettered by concepts of being or non-being, of manifestation or potential, all enlightened qualities unfold automatically. Without using fancy jargon, the accomplishers of the Karma Kagyu school express this truth about meditation and life in the following way: "If nothing outer or inner appears, this is mind's space-essence, its possibilities. When something appears, be it inner experiences or outer worlds, this is its clarity-nature, mind's free play. The fact that both can happen, space and what occurs in it, is its unlimited expression." This is a modern way of conveying Buddha's view. Two thousand five hundred and fifty years ago, he taught his more conceptual students about sixteen levels of emptiness or the non-reality of events. The ones who were so close to him that they could understand intuitively, he told: "Form is emptiness, emptiness is form. Form and emptiness are inseparable." He put his ultimate wisdom into the world where it still lives today. Whoever sees that everything is mind can only act joyfully and spontaneously. All **"roots of illusion"** will have been **"cut away."**

Only the obstacles to enlightenment are removable. The boundless, radiant space of perfect awareness can neither be improved, nor may any truth be taken from it. Although over thousands of years people have attempted to intellectually comprehend it, the state of the eternal here and now appears through one's openness to the lama's blessing and manifests when most veils and concepts have been cut through. In spite of the examples of so many great accomplishers throughout history, these seem to be difficult points to fulfill. This total and fastest way to accomplishment calls for a really clear conscience or unbroken bonds so one can let go of any manipulation and instead simply trust space. Of course logical thinking and mental training also have their functions towards this end, as do all other mental capacities that are the gifts of space to itself. They guide and inspire on the way and round things off. In addition, a clear understanding of the teachings and massive pleasant impressions in one's store-consciousness permit the deep relaxation that then changes into a lasting experience of mind. A rather corny joke from my childhood near Copenhagen neatly explains what is best avoided: A man is looking for something underneath a street-lamp at night. A friend asks what is happening and the answer is: "I've lost my key." The friend says, "Where?" and the man points, "Over there." "Then why are you looking here?" he asks and his friend says, "Because this is where the light is."

Whoever searches for mind through its thoughts, concepts, and feelings is like this man looking for his keys. One doesn't understand that it is the seeker that is sought. Mind sees and perceives itself. Therefore Karmapa's fervent wish is that beings find the **"root of illusion."** The more one contemplates and opens up to the world on the basis of this insight, the more meaningless any dualistic view or behavior becomes. Manifestation and space are then two sides of the same totality, and it is seen to express its endless richness through whatever may appear and not appear. Although many would prefer to avoid surprises by reading books and accessing this wisdom intellectually, it is only after meeting a holder of this realization that the view and experience of enlightenment will spread compellingly over all levels of one's totality and give them ultimate meaning. The power of meeting with the holder of a well developed "both-and" awareness is so intense and fulfilling that any fears about opening up can dissolve and even the highest abilities of discrimination and clear thinking can unite with the moment of direct perception.

Today, representatives of the Diamond Way manifest this effortless transformation of any situation into self-arisen joy. For those who know teachers on this level, they are convincing proof that enlightenment is unshakable, unlimited, and beyond all concepts. One feels something deeply precious, all encompassing and powerful—a real refuge.

Maitripa, 1007–77

ཡོད་པ་མ་ཡིན་རྒྱལ་བས་ཀྱང་མ་གཟིགས་སོ།།

May we recognize mind's essence, which is free of any extremes.

མེད་པ་མ་ཡིན་འཁོར་འདས་ཀུན་གྱི་གཞི།།

It is not existent, for even the buddhas do not see it.

འགལ་འདུ་མ་ཡིན་ཟུང་འཇུག་དབུ་མའི་ལམ།།

It is not non-existent, for it is the basis of everything, of conditioned existence and of the state beyond suffering.

མཐའ་བྲལ་སེམས་ཀྱི་ཆོས་ཉིད་རྟོགས་པར་ཤོག།

This is no contradiction. It is the middle way of unity.

Verse 11

Once again, just a few lines express a complete philosophy in a precise and perfect style. Karmapa's simple words are enlightened insights and point directly to mind's timeless essence.

In the Kagyu lineage a teacher will stretch himself to impart the liberating teachings in the most useful way to his students. In this verse, however, Karmapa follows a more typical approach. He transmits the essential insight into mind's nature by first pointing to its space-essence. To make this possible, he begins by removing any stiff ideas concerning the nature of reality and enables everyone to see the essential freedom that is beyond the concepts of being and non-being. The richness of resting in the moment of direct experience and being at home with whatever happens is indescribable. Many powerful experiences now come into being and one must handle a rich but rounded lifestyle. Growth is like driving a racing car: if you wipe out on the curve, then you were going too fast; but if you didn't, then you were going too slowly. It is therefore understandable and well appreciated that on the direct approach of the Great Seal all growth takes place inside the protective field supplied by the refuge!

Mind cannot be established as being material; it cannot be experienced as a something. In north India 2,550 years ago, the young prince Siddharta Gautama reached enlightenment by recognizing that no own, separate mind can be found. Thus any obstacles through ignorance or disturbing feelings like expectation, fear, attachment, and aversion simply fell away; and the unhindered unfolding of his mind made him a Buddha. As any investigation shows mind to be without weight, form, color, taste, or size, Buddha described it as being essentially "empty," i.e., empty of any such characteristics. At that time, this term must have been appropriate, but today saying that it is not a thing, or even more so, that it is space-like seems to fit and excite more people. Mathematicians tend to see it as the neutral element and physicists as potential. The Japanese typically speak of there being "no mind," focusing on its basic space-awareness that cannot be found. The Tibetans, especially those of the three old schools, are fascinated by its clarity and the playful power it expresses. As something is clearly felt to be experiencing, we speak of "mind." It is two sides of the same coin. Everything happens all the time. Outside as well as inside oneself, worlds and experiences manifest, express their potential, are known, and disappear. The fact that both space and its content can exist is no contradiction, but rather proves mind's unlimited quality, uniting everything.

Whoever focuses on mind as space will become fearless. Whatever is not a thing cannot be destroyed. This of course does not imply that one should uncritically make mistakes or jump without a parachute, throwing one's life away. Instead, this insight brings about a trustworthy fearlessness that goes to the marrow of one's bones. One recognizes, beyond any doubt, that what experiences all the impermanent phenomena is itself indestructible and that the space around and between one's thoughts and feelings is not limited by space or time. The experience, that mind is in essence space, lets this absolute certainty arise.

And why does this self-evident realization change people to such a high degree? Because without it, one does not have a reliable refuge and is unprotected in life. At the beginning of someone's spiritual development, nearly everyone identifies with being their body. This view, however, means that disease, old age, death, and loss are real—and so is the unavoidability of suffering. If, for these reasons, one wishes to identify differently and instead prefers to be one's thoughts and feelings, then little is gained! Being conditioned, they change rapidly and have no independent or lasting existence. No matter how hard one tries, pleasant states cannot be kept; and fighting bad feelings is frustrating as they just gain in energy.

The recognition that mind is indestructible and provides boundless opportunities, transforms the richness of its expressions into spontaneous joy. Then outer as well as inner manifestations become its free play, and everything is continually fresh and new. Its awareness-nature unites and encompasses everyone and one acts in the here and now from this wisdom. For a while, confusion and conditioned views may still appear. They are not taken seriously, but rather are allowed to play a bit and then dissolve back into limitless space. Therefore Karmapa describes mind as **"not existent"** and also **"not non-existent."**

What unites, beyond contradiction, these two statements about mind? The realization that both space and clarity are two inseparable sides of the same unlimited essence. In the **"middle way of unity"** and the non-stick, non-gluey nirvana, which is beyond confusion and attachment to only peace, the previous lines reach their completion. They show mind's limitless expression. Although it can only be described as boundless and conscious space, it still contains and experiences everything. The recognition that this is so leads one to enlightenment, while the inability to realize this is the fundamental ignorance of all unenlightened beings. It makes them consider transient states to be permanent and causes the suffering of the conditioned world.

Whoever stays conscious of the mirror behind the changing pictures and does not forget the timeless ocean underneath the waves has reached the goal. As one never loses the taste of the experiencer during the flow of countless experiences, there is no place for doubt; and one will constantly benefit beings. Watching all events with amusement, one is freed; and no power is lost to expectation or fear. The aim of the view and the meditations of the Diamond Way is to accomplish exactly this.

Marpa, 1012–97

འདི་ཡིན་ཞེས་པ་གང་གིས་མཚོན་པ་མེད། །

May we find certainty in the ultimate true meaning:

འདི་མིན་ཞེས་བྱ་གང་གིས་བཀག་པ་མེད། །

One cannot prove it by saying "it is this."

བློ་ལས་འདས་པའི་ཆོས་ཉིད་འདུས་མ་བྱས། །

One cannot deny it by saying "it is not that."

ཡང་དག་དོན་གྱི་མཐའ་ནི་ངེས་པར་ཤོག །

Truth nature, beyond concepts, is non-composite.

Verse 12

Karmapa here continues the broad flow of Great Seal experience concerning mind. Being the essential instructions of the Kagyu lineage, they aim at direct experience and should neither be over-interpreted nor remain unclear. By dissolving the concepts that block one's immediate experience of unity, he brings the vibrant qualities of his statements to their full maturation.

This verse is a venerable seven hundred years old but still manages to feel completely modern, and again Karmapa stresses the main liberating points. Mind cannot be described as a something because it has no material characteristics. However, because of the steady flow of experiences, it also cannot be denied. Scenarios unfold constantly, both inside and outside, and are felt by unenlightened beings to be real. Mind, as an experiencer, is timeless space. Whatever appears then changes, is observed by mind, and disappears again in mind's clarity. The fact that both exist simultaneously, in constant exchange and without obstruction, shows its unlimited expression. Mind can only recognize itself from a state beyond concepts. This takes place most quickly through the boundless feelings of thankfulness, confidence, and openness, known as devotion. Such joyful striving towards fulfillment allows less and less space for expectation and fear. Thus concepts of being and non-being have their roots destroyed, and mind recognizes itself.

No more convincing exponent of this all-inclusive way of transformation could be found than the great accomplisher

Milarepa. Although he started his career nine hundred and fifty years ago by killing thirty-five enemies on his sweet mother's request, after thirty years of active involvement with the methods and view of the Diamond Way he was able to disappear at death into a rainbow. During his life he compared himself to a drunken elephant that acts without concepts and has no fear. He helped countless beings on their way to enlightenment. Acting directly and without pretense, he was always in the here and now.

But why does Karmapa use several verses to explain the same points? Because they are all so vital. There exists no other perfection than knowing one's own mind, and a conceptual understanding will in no way suffice. Only a meaningful repetition of these indispensable basic truths will implant them with sufficient power in one's consciousness and bring about that trustworthy maturity, which makes one a refuge for others.

It is not difficult to ascertain that one is still on one's way to a totally dependable inner state. Despite the recognition that any lasting happiness can only be found in mind and is in itself a product of massive good karma, inner weaknesses will continue to manifest on one's way. The main disturbing factor for unenlightened beings is the mistaken perception that one is a "self" separated from the totality, that there exists a lasting and real "me." Thus instead of relaxing into the richness of space, this illusion brings about attempts to embellish the imagined me with lasting relative qualities, which is impossible, as they are essentially passing.

In this race some people want to be brave and may therefore go skydiving, enjoy a wild partner, or ride a fast motorcycle. Others understand the great importance of generosity and support their Diamond Way center or some other worthy cause. If someone wants to develop wisdom, they usually go out and buy some books on philosophy. Any attempt, however, to add selected qualities to this non-existent me will bring only limited benefit. Working to develop partial improvements of a mind that is out there, that one's illusory self hopes to manifest or identify with when needed or possible, produces a picture with little balance; and in particular there will be a great deal of indecisiveness. At the farmers' market of one's mind, one will be constantly trading blind horses for toothless ones and vice versa. If one is thinking, "If I accept this quality as mine, then I will have to give up this other interesting one, which I am already rather used to," then little of a meaningful nature can be gained. For example one may notice with anguish that the physical courage one developed helps little when a friend is sick. Eventually maturity will make it clear that one read some really superficial spiritual books! And that mixing the terminologies and information offered was the most stupid thing one could have done. Any attempt to transform a non-existent self or I into a "spiritual self" or an "elevated I" removes beings from their center. Even with the most constant endeavor it is impossible to perfect all things through one's will alone. Conditions change all the time. Reality, however, beyond concepts, is timeless and not composite.

A deep trust in the here and now thus brings all things to complete fruition. One may add this exquisite roof of highest view when the necessary foundation of useful behavior has hardened and the walls of a meaningful motivation have been erected. One's growing recognition here is that highest truth means timeless bliss, power, confidence, and love and that all perfect qualities appear spontaneously from luminous space when one does not obstruct it. Beyond any doubt, all beings and oneself are understood to share an essential awareness. All possess a buddha nature that simply has not yet been recognized—where one is constantly surrounded by a realm of highest bliss and where every particle vibrates with joy and is kept together by love. On the level of the Diamond Way, nobody needs to go elsewhere to meet the Buddhas or to die in order to enter a pure land; purifying one's view is sufficient! Even the sweetest expectations or the most pleasant daydream fades alongside the richness of what is actually present. From that moment of highest insight and on, all its inherent perfections appear without end.

But what exactly is this absolute meaning called enlightenment? As Karmapa dedicated twenty-five verses in its honor, here are a few additional statements:

The Great Seal is actually nothing but the steady, conscious and uninhibited expression of a purified and fully functioning mind. Its basis is all beings' timeless buddha essence, that mind is clear light. The ways to this state start at the level of a clear awareness concerning cause and effect, move through the development of compassion and wisdom, and arrive at oneness with enlightenment. If possible they will also have been empowered by the turbo-charged highest pure view of the Diamond Way. The goal reached is the self-liberating, effortless expression of the full potential of space; and its accomplishment manifests as the three levels, the four activities, and the five wisdoms mentioned earlier. And how does this mental state express itself in life? When one has recognized mind's essence to be space, one's style of behavior will express insight and deep security. Joy and thankfulness, which appear without any outer cause, show mind's experience of its own infinite nature and expresses itself through an active compassion that is full of humor and directed towards preserving the freedom of beings and life's other most valuable qualities.

Whoever reaches enlightenment will act without any perception of a separation between subject, object, and action.

Depending on beings' needs and always in order to develop their long-term potential, one expresses the peace-giving activity when people are licking their wounds, the increasing one when they feel expansive, the fascinating one when they have enough success and surplus to share, and the powerful protective activities when they recognize their strength..

The enlightened wisdoms also appear spontaneously, without any effort. They are nothing but an insightful understanding into one's disturbing feelings and the use of their energies. As their transformation is so important for beings' daily well being, this process should be mentioned once again. When the feelings are allowed to pass without being acted upon, the essence of anger is seen to be a state of mirror-like awareness, showing things as they are; and pride becomes a wisdom, which equalizes and expresses the many-sided richness of all things. Attachment gives one the power to discriminate, understanding things singly and as parts of a totality. Jealousy produces all-performing wisdom, making one able to make a sequence out of historical facts or one's experiences. And finally, as the clouds of ignorance empty of rain, even confusion becomes all-pervading insight. It is therefore not difficult to understand why Karmapa promotes this absolute meaning as the true goal.

འདི་ཉིད་མ་རྟོགས་འཁོར་བའི་རྒྱ་མཚོར་འཁོར།

As long as this is not realized, one drifts in the ocean of
conditioned existence.

འདི་ཉིད་རྟོགས་ན་སངས་རྒྱས་གཞན་ན་མེད།

When it is recognized, buddhahood is nothing else.

ཐམས་ཅད་འདི་ཡིན་འདི་མིན་གང་ཡང་མེད།

Then there is no "it is this, it is not that."

ཆོས་ཉིད་ཀུན་གཞིའི་མཚང་ནེ་རིག་པར་ཤོག

May we reveal the truth-nature, the hidden basis of everything.

VERSE 13

One's experiences of conditioned worlds, as well as the frustrations felt by beings, have only one cause: that unenlightened mind does not experience itself. Whoever does not see the mirror behind its pictures or fails to recognize the ocean underneath its waves will consider conditioned and transitory events to be real. Mind will then be attracted or repulsed by its pleasant or difficult experiences and waste its power producing expectation and fear. There is then no way it can free itself from the limitations of past and future.

Unable to recognize that experiencer, object experienced and the act of experiencing are in constant interaction and constitute different sides of the same totality, mind's space-essence, its awareness, will experience being an "I." Thus it will consider its clarity and free play, as something separate, as a "you." From this illusory experience of duality the basic disturbing feelings of confusion, attachment, and ill will appear. They trigger further painful conditions such as greed, jealousy, and the harmful, exclusive kind of pride that is the total opposite of the diamond-like, inclusive pride of enjoying the good in others. As mentioned before, Buddha speaks of eighty-four thousand possible combinations of these basic faults and gave the same number of teachings to combat them. Objectively viewed, the experience of conflicting emotions is mind's self-purification, as is all other pain. Through them, one is actually freed of impressions that burden one. If one manages to let such states pass without acting upon them and producing fresh causes of trouble, then their effect is to liberate mind. Thus although unpleasant, their appearance may be welcomed as a purification of one's subconscious; and a mature observation of their nature produces the experience to benefit others in similar situations.

The tricky point with disturbing emotions is that for a long time one considers their transient plays to be real and acts upon them. This is the case right up until liberation. If not purified, the unwholesome seeds they sow in body, speech, and mind will later bring about outer and inner difficulties. When they do appear—and they will if not removed by meditation or other conscious means—one will not recognize their unreal nature. Once again one will act from a state of delusion. One will harm others or oneself through clumsy words and actions and will lack the power to break out of the conditioned cycle.

As long as mind's all-pervading nature is not understood, every experience will be colored by one's education, culture, and emotional state and must remain inside the realm of time and place. Because mind is here limited to the flow of experiences and lacks awareness of its own timeless space, the chain of conditioned rebirths will not be broken. Even the happiest of unenlightened beings do not rest in their own perfect essence. They are not totally satisfied simply through their own power. They grasp for happiness and try to avoid losing it. It is impossible, however, for anything conditioned to be stable and lasting.

"When it is recognized, buddhahood is nothing else."

Realizing non-ego, that there is no self in either body or mind, means immediate liberation. This is the end of any limiting experience of duality, and all disturbing feelings will unravel by themselves. Clumsy words and actions thus lose their roots; and our own habitual lapses, as well as any strange

106

behavior by others, are noticed with bemused detachment. Instead, all of mind's timeless and perfect qualities begin to appear and are known to be absolute. On one's way to enlightenment, the realization becomes certainty that this space-awareness is indestructible. Thus one's growing experience that mind expresses unending richness and cannot be obstructed in its expression can allow all expectation and fear to fall away. As mind recognizes its luminous power ever more strongly behind its changing objects, its fearless omniscience, self-arisen joy and active compassion will manifest; buddhahood is nothing but this. Everything conditioned is in a state of constant flux. Being and non-being, appearance and non-appearance express the same totality. Therefore neither the outer nor the inner worlds can be fathomed through the view of "either-or." Whereas on the relative level one must act as if the conditioned world of the senses that one is sharing with others is real, the absolute view that everything outer and inner are the joyful play of a limitless potential is never lost.

Buddha himself saw the world of the senses as an illusion and compared it to a dream, a rainbow or a water-bubble. A modern view would understand all outer phenomena as being a frame, condensed out of space from the countless common inclinations of beings. It is then additionally interpreted through the colored glasses of beings' private and changing attitudes. Both are karmic—they are conditioned through cause and effect—and one can free oneself from them. This dissolution of one's own emotional coloring of the world is the state called liberation or the small nirvana, while the additional disappearance of all stiff concepts is enlightenment. Here mind works and enjoys without any hindrance.

Thus everything is mind. Seen from the absolute view of the Great Seal, both the free play of the potential of space and the limited perceptions of beings are expressions of that same source. They are the karmas, the tendencies, and the changing moods of beings condensing out of space and also what they experience in connection with that. Resting in the awareness that neither the world of appearance nor the personal filters through which it is perceived have any solidity, one comes to realize that in essence mind is clear light, radiant, and naturally energetic. This leads to the experience that subject, object, and action are interdependent and that restrictions in time and place exist only on the relative level. Leaving out all limited views is perfection; and whoever needs neither to prove nor to excuse anything but spontaneously expresses mind's richness on all levels has already accomplished the goal.

No wonder that Karmapa wishes this for all beings!

When Buddha's students were mature as human beings and had real questions, he joyfully passed on his highest wisdom, the teachings of the Diamond Way. If they were precocious, however, or just wanted to show their learnedness by saying something, he quickly went back to basics. Once he answered a typical new-age type question like this: "What would you do if you were hit by a poisoned arrow? Would you ask who shot you, what his family was like, where he lived, or would you pull the arrow out?" Upon receiving the expected answer, Buddha continued: "But you were shot. You were born and therefore you will surely die. What will you now do with the time you have? Ask many questions about subjects that can never help you, or take the arrow out? Now bring your mind to a state where old age, sickness, and death cannot harm you."

Milarepa, 1052–1135

སྣང་ཡང་སེམས་ལ་སྟོང་ཡང་སེམས་ཡིན་ཏེ།

Appearance is mind and so is emptiness.

རྟོགས་ཀྱང་སེམས་ལ་འཁྲུལ་ཡང་རང་གི་སེམས།

Realization is mind and so is delusion.

སྐྱེས་ཀྱང་སེམས་ལ་འགགས་ཀྱང་སེམས་ཡིན་པས།

All phenomena arising and ceasing are mind.

བློ་འདོགས་ཐམས་ཅད་སེམས་ལ་ཆོད་པར་ཤོག།

May we cut through all affirmations and doubts concerning mind.

VERSE 14

Once again Karmapa points to the limitless space of experience that is beyond contradiction. Everything is mind, whether or not it can be comprehended through thoughts or imagination. From continually new angles he elucidates that whoever rests in his own essence already has everything. Whoever isn't stuck in tomorrow or yesterday has every insight and will express meaningful, self-arisen activity. Over time, no ego can withstand the growing certainty that one can trust space, that all is in essence true and fulfils itself effortlessly. Thus the realm of the self disintegrates and mind's spontaneous qualities appear naturally as enlightenment. As with several earlier verses, Karmapa again mentions the object perceived before the space that is perceiving; he places mind's joyful expression ahead of the truth-level from which it springs.

"Appearance" indicates mind's clarity, its richness and versatility. No matter how real experiences may seem to be, there is nothing that can stay. Everything is conditioned and composite, whether observed from inside or out. In the same way that every act of perception returns to space, so too the material universe itself is like the former Bank of Italy. The non-existence of one lira also meant that billions of lira were an illusion. Similarly, the seemingly solid universe has no fundamental and timeless particle from which it arose. In a particle accelerator or cyclotron matter can be made to disappear. This is one sign that the world is not fixed or truly existent, and one day it will probably be possible to prove that it has the characteristics of the collective dream described in an earlier chapter.

"Emptiness" characterizes mind's space-essence, its timeless basis. The term points to the experiencer and its potential, to that which may happen. Its width enables it to contain all possibilities. No karma or other stored impressions can limit it. It is, was, and will always be free.

"Realization" is mind. Here the word describes the condition where mind knows its own essence, where mind's eye looks into the mirror and frees itself. It is the state where it becomes conscious of the ocean underneath the waves; and the experiencer recognizes itself as timeless, clear light. At this moment, mind's unobstructed qualities radiate forth. Undisturbed by outer influences or inner concepts, they will constantly make it clear that enlightenment is nothing but mind's realization of its emptiness, clarity, and unlimited essence.

The term **"delusion"** represents the mental states before mind recognizes its absolute qualities. Here the timeless mirror is not seen but only its images. Whoever lives without the absolute refuge of aware and compassionate space will consider transient experiences as well as one's own ideas to be real and will waver as they come and go. In that situation one is like an eye that only notices the impressions it receives but is unaware of itself. Because all things continually change, depending on the ripening of our own and collective karmas, this is not a recipe for finding anything of a lasting nature. Though one only reaps what one has sown oneself through body, speech, and mind, the results ripen at uncertain times and carry over from life to life. It is for this reason that people often consider life unjust and remain confused.

"Arising" expresses mind's free play, the expression of its abilities. This power is used in mind-expanding ways during the building-up phase of the Diamond Way meditations from the point where the Buddha is invoked, whose qualities one wishes to obtain. From such levels of beyond-personal purity, known as *Kye Rim*, or the birth of the buddha aspect, one's arrival at the state of truth is much easier than attempting the steps from beings' everyday emotional consciousness.

"Ceasing" means the self-liberating return to space of phenomena and perceptions. If one can remain aware during this process without being dependent on outer or inner support structures, this is all-pervading insight. In Diamond Way meditations this is accomplished through a successful completion phase, during which the buddha or lama meditated upon melts together with the practitioner and an identification of body, speech, and mind takes place. The ensuing experience of radiating timeless space is called *dzog rim* or the state of perfection. One should only practice this for as long as mind is radiant like a diamond. If it becomes dull like a white wall, one must stop immediately. Otherwise one will lose one's fangs and become unable to act decisively.

Two thousand five hundred and fifty years ago, Buddha clarified the ultimate nature of things in what is today a well-known quotation; **"Form is emptiness, emptiness is form, form and emptiness are inseparable."** This highest teaching existed during the first fifteen hundred years in northern India under the name of Maha-mudra, Maha-ati, or Maha-madhyamaka, until the Muslims destroyed that civilization. Then one thousand years ago the instructions, now under the names of Chag Chen, Dzog Chen or Uma Chenpo were brought to Tibet by the hero Marpa and others. Today the idealistic and educated Western world is uniquely capable of holding this level of awareness that has now, in the Kagyu Lineage, been translated into "The Great Seal." It seeks the realization that experiencer and experience, space and phenomena, arise dependently but at the same time have no nature or lasting characteristics of their own and that mind's unlimited qualities make everything possible. These factors, which should be evident also in daily life when one has been made aware of them, are complementary aspects of the essential state. They unite fearless truth with self-arisen joy and the powerful compassionate actions that come from honest forward thinking. They are like humidity, clouds, and rain: all essentially water.

In the awareness-field of the accomplishers, beyond **"all affirmations and doubts concerning mind,"** mind constantly and effortlessly unfolds its qualities. Nothing could be nobler than that. Therefore Karmapa repeatedly underlines the fact that mind is the source of everything. In its essence it is self-arisen enlightenment, a state that was always inherent in it. Whatever manifests inside or out appears from the space of mind, unfolds there, is known through its awareness, and dissolves back into its boundlessness. Karmapa advises us to utilize this process without hesitation on the level of practical living, benefiting beings with a relaxed confidence in the indestructible and essential perfection of what acts and experiences.

This certainty of mind's essence, which is in principle faultless, is the basis for true greatness. The insight that beneath the wildest surf, or behind the most exciting images, the timeless power of the ocean and the mirror are even more meaningful and radiant, remains the guiding light for the three old or Red Hat schools of Tibetan Buddhism. Their way works towards the experience of space and joy as inseparable—the so-called *Shentong* view—through enlightened feedback systems for body, speech, and mind. Because of these highly effective methods of meditation and the necessary bond to one's experienced lama, they can press countless buttons in people's store-consciousness. A few years meditating on the buddha forms with this disposition bring about changes that would have taken many lives if one had only studied or thought that space was simply neutral. Because the Diamond Way activates beings' totality and harnesses feelings, urges, instincts, and dreams in the process, the robustly joyful and much sought after complete human maturity develops quickly. Thus mind's timeless essence is experienced; and one deeply knows what is behind and between thoughts, what the basis of all things brings forth and can do. With an indestructible feeling of bliss one here discovers that mind is totally free. It can be conscious without needing an object, just resting in itself; the perfect qualities of what experiences can in no way be removed. Whoever can obtain and skillfully benefit from a teacher and teachings that make such experiences possible, should celebrate. In the long run, their happiness will only increase!

How then can one **"cut through all affirmations and doubts concerning mind"** that steal the freshness of the immediate experience? Buddha calls for an attack on sleepiness and habits that engages our outer, inner, and secret qualities. In short it means to outwardly avoid what harms others and inwardly to develop a rich treasure of compassion and wisdom. On the secret and ultimate level of view, he tells us to have the courage to behave like him.

A meaningful Buddhist life would imply being aware on these three levels simultaneously and, where possible, to work from the highest point of view. Knowing the moment of original freshness to be true, the first "a-ha" of an exciting insight should not be assessed, intellectualized, or evaluated. Although this may not be easy—coming from cultures that operate with sin, the will of gods, and other similar concepts that destroy beings' immediate confidence in the moment of experience—one should leave the radiant newness of every reasonable event undisturbed and simply BE. While on the Diamond Way, the state of immediate, unfiltered awareness is gradually made to stay without constraint. At the same time, however, one is aware of one's remaining karmic conditioning, the limitations of one's senses, local customs and one's mental habits. Therefore one uses mind's knowledge and freedom to harmonize what happened or was seen with the absolute teachings on the nature of things. In this way, relative and absolute levels of awareness are made to supplement and enhance one another for the benefit of many.

The timeless radiance of the moment must not fade while the conditioned world is freely enjoyed. From the depth of one's heart one enjoys the rich variety of self-arisen events. Experienced from this level, each of these is of deep meaning and manifests the potential of space. It is then one's commitment, however, to simultaneously carry the toolbox of worldly wisdoms at one's side. One is now responsible for improving the conditioned world as durably as possible from the position of a meaningful and liberated point of view. As long as beings mistake their changing situations to be real and experience conditioned happiness and suffering through them, this approach is important. As mentioned previously, doing useful things and avoiding harmful actions in one's life is only sensible. Although mind is in essence timeless and everything manifesting is impermanent, one can still wake-up from a good dream into liberation and enlightenment. Whoever fills mind with negative actions, words, and motivation, however, will find mind equally amazing in its ability to produce more and more pain.

Nothing is truer than the unaffected stream of naked richness experienced by a fearless mind. It contains all love and adventures. Here separation, past and future, dissolve in the moment of feeling the power of what is possible. When one is certain of observing things with a minimum of disturbing feelings, statements like "first thought–best thought" or rather "first intuition–best intuition" become meaningful. This is because thoughts entail a partial transformation of one's experience and this forces happiness to have a certain distance to a situation.

As many know, Buddha's teaching is simply the way things are—without dogmas or any other form of coercion. Therefore intelligent doubt and critical observation help massively towards its realization. Through investigation, one comprehends life on more and more levels. In addition, proven facts sharpen the tools of the teachings and enable them to encompass any event. This makes it easy to help others later. If nothing remains unresolved, then the development of students is not disturbed by unclear statements or information that cannot be verified.

For self-reliant people who want to live without divine supervision, difficulties with Buddhism mainly appear from a lack of knowledge. One must have either learnt too little or too partially—or tried to incorporate things that did not fit one's capacity. On each level the goal of Buddha's teachings is always the same—his students should not believe but know. He gave instructions for people to become independent and, if possible, enlightened. One's awareness of what is absolute or remains relative will translate into fearless, exciting, and kind forms of activity.

For this reason, everything stilted and artificial misses the point. Such behavior limits awareness and strength. Every spontaneously arising insight, however, is a fleeting glance at enlightenment and sets one free. Therefore one may use and enjoy relative thoughts, but they should not be considered too real. If they set in motion processes of hope and fear, one is deeply in the conditioned world. Outside the feeling that we truly grow and develop, there exists nothing completely satisfactory. Whoever does not trust space here and now, may hardly ever notice the self-liberating potential that constantly manifests in the situations of one's life.

Being the boundless moment of awareness—and no alternative way to enlightenment ever existed—makes it possible to experience all things from one's center. Thus one knows beyond any doubt that space is information, bliss and active compassion, and that it timelessly encompasses and unites all things.

Gampopa, 1079–1153

བློས་བྱས་རྩོལ་བའི་སྒོམ་ཁྲིས་མ་བསླད་ཅིང་།

Unpolluted by deliberate and intellectual meditation,

ཐ་མལ་འདུ་འཛིའི་རླུང་གིས་མ་བསྐྱོད་པར།

and not driven by the winds of ordinary life:

མ་བཅོས་གཉུག་མ་རང་བབ་འཇོག་ཤེས་པའི།

may we learn to rest mind in its non-artificial and natural state

སེམས་དོན་ཉམས་ལེན་མཁས་ཤིང་སྐྱོང་བར་ཤོག།

and be skilled in sustaining this practice of mind's nature.

VERSE 15

This verse starts in a dramatic manner. **"Polluted"** is a powerful word in the mouth of an enlightened teacher and it points to a high state of alertness. Karmapa's next words focus on the exact hindrances that block the perfection and happiness of unenlightened beings.

After the joyful realization of the last few verses that everything is mind, the objective here is to receive the experience and fortify what has been established. In the first two lines, Karmapa brings to light the serious obstacles to effective meditation, mind's tightness and its distractibility and then continues by explaining how an accomplisher can turn every experience into a step towards enlightenment.

What is the **"deliberate and intellectual meditation"** he mentions? Seen through the eyes of the Diamond Way it is not meditation at all but contemplation or deep thinking. In a state of meditation, one does not try to produce anything but instead rests consciously in the perception of what is. Thus one stays in the center of the powerfields invoked, remains without stress in the multiplicity of what is going on, and feels joyful and conscious during the moment of experience. Here nothing must be excused nor proven, neither clinging nor avoiding would have any meaning. One is aware and at home in the present with all senses open, naturally one with what is.

True reflection recognizes mind's beginningless vastness. Beyond all imagination and doubt, one understands that awareness is essentially space. One then realizes that every event expresses its clarity, its free play. The final insight that both these are its unlimited manifestation is then enlightenment. No longer seeking restlessly for moments of joy through further distractions, which some consider the pinnacle of happiness, mind radiates through its own power. Its luminosity is nothing but its inherent power of awareness. It appears inseparably from the experience itself.

In true meditation, thoughts are no enemy. Whatever their contents may be, one notices them appear naturally as mind's richness, remains relaxed as they move by and stays aware as they dissolve back into space, watching them like children playing. If mind did not have its thoughts, it would simply be poorer! If they produce neither disturbing feelings nor unwieldy concepts, thoughts thus bring no harm. If nothing distracting is experienced, it is awareness that counts. Staying in the here and now, mind is like a glass of muddy water in which the particles gradually settle. Its power of consciousness needs nothing from elsewhere and handles outer as well as inner events with decreasing aberration. As mind's understanding of itself, in particular the view of the Great Seal, is essential on the Diamond Way, here are some further comments on the first line of this verse. What actually happens during a meditation? Conscious space appears! Over ever longer periods of time and with increasing conviction, space will be known as that which is behind and between events and which understands them. In this way, one recognizes it to be the timeless basis of all things and true in essence. Liberating insights and Buddhas appear without effort as an expression of its inherent enlightenment. Wherever mind recognizes itself, its boundless space is realized.

There are fundamental differences between these Buddhist methods and views and those of other religions although bleeding hearts, spiritually lazy people, and those disinclined to read and discriminate don't want to know about it. One-pointed Hindu meditations and their striving towards will-power or a thoughtless state as well as Christian contemplation, which aims to drill-in certain thought patterns and fill one's mind with what one wishes to later believe, are totally different from what Buddhists do. The Great Seal works without coercion. It builds on a conscious, nonjudgmental way of letting impressions pass. The experiencer recognizes itself through effortlessly remaining in what is. In Northern or Great Way Buddhism deep contemplation is an important tool for learning but in the Diamond Way this practice is not considered meditation. It is seen as belonging to the level of working with concepts but is not frowned upon. Contemplation of ideas is a useful means for sorting through information and analyzing facts. Through it, one may engage in vast learning structures on the level of inner collectedness but not in an intuitive manner.

Thinking as well as any reliance on concepts during meditation is not advised for the Great Seal and Diamond Way practices. They may remove the selfish and conceptual obstacles to mind's realization but lack the power of involving body, speech, mind and all one's other inherent qualities. It is like when a finger points to the moon. Although the direction is hopefully correct, the finger itself is not the moon. Concepts make one look for mind in a way that it cannot be found. Because this tendency easily sneaks into beings' meditation, striking especially immature students or those who are dissatisfied with their lives, Karmapa goes as far as using this word **"pollution."** He advises enlightening meditations beyond words and daydreaming that use systems of feedback and naked awareness to develop body, speech, and mind. Both the self-liberating insights of the Great Seal and the countless Buddha-forms of the Diamond Way meditations appear spontaneously from the inherent wisdom of space. If they correspond to Buddha's Diamond Way teachings and the forms of energy and light transmitted through blessing and initiations, one can completely trust them. They are mind's spontaneous richness and need no further confirmation. Used in the powerfield of a lama who embodies the aware space behind any duality, the possibility of such enlightened potential becomes evident. If one adds strong motivation through the Four Thoughts that begin every meditation and turn mind towards lasting values, to a level of human maturity developed through the refuge and a sturdy grounding from the Foundational Practices, then one's basis is truly solid. On that background any meditation on the Diamond Way level should unfold automatically and without needing any force. Naturally one brings mind back from an escapade, like when one shows a child where it should be, but there is no need for drama. On the Diamond Way, one's progress towards enlightenment is like a sexist joke about meeting a beautiful woman. If one runs after her she will call the police. But if one parks one's Porsche and places a checkbook on the roof she will come by herself.

Thoughts, including the most disturbing kinds, are mind's free play and are actually a joyful expression of its power. Used as a means to find beyond-personal truth, however, they can only point to the possibility of enlightened states or remove conceptual obstacles to their realization. The actual experiencer of mind is far beyond their scope. The moment one gives reality to thoughts, one's meditation needs first aid. Although thoughts are useful for the relative affairs of life, during Diamond Way meditations they have no function. Here experiencer, experience and object experienced become one and all-encompassing awareness is all that remains. Already in the earlier verses Karmapa warned against conceptual thinking during meditation, here he extends his warning to everything forced, cramped, or narrow. Effortless abiding stops when a part of mind becomes the policeman who assesses what is meditating.

The Great Seal should be boundless like deep love. One should feel like during the free fall before one's parachute opens or when taking a fast motorcycle down a curvy road with no speed traps. Its object is mind's experience of its own timeless essence, not the flow of its contents. There is no greater joy. It transcends all concepts, is known to be more real than anything else, and encompasses every cell in one's body. One's wish to employ one's own experience for the benefit of all, and the certainty that aware space is indestructible makes possible a courageous, beyond personal and completely liberating view. With this confidence unpleasant experiences become both instructions on how to help others and purifications that dissolve the causes of severe later sufferings while everything pleasant becomes a blessing to share with others. Thus, step-by-step, mind gets to better know itself. Using the Great Seal one doesn't only get older, which beings manage anyway, but surely also wiser.

"Not driven by the winds."

An accomplisher like Karmapa whose oneness with mind's experience of space is unmarred and timeless, will first notice beings' inner disturbances. They ultimately cause the outer hindrances and are felt to be very real for a long time. He also knows very clearly what triggers such states on a daily basis, the confusion or **"winds of ordinary life."** Such inner situations and the expectation and fear they engender have great power and last till one reaches the level where everything conditioned is recognized to be dream-like and impermanent. This important state of liberation is followed by increasing steps towards enlightenment, with the ever-more profound view of the Great Seal, providing basis, way, and goal. Everything, including every disturbance, is transformed ever more into mind's play and free expression. Through such factors, it mirrors and recognizes both the level of awareness reached and also its relevance as an expression of highest wisdom. Each incident is seen as a teaching, as continually new means, projected by mind in order to recognize its boundlessness. Thus even the habitual activities of an unconscious lifestyle stop being experienced as meaningless. Instead, they become a conscious motor for development and strength.

Getting born, working, paying taxes, and dying; the practitioner cannot avoid chores like these. He also makes love, eats, and dresses so that his body brings pleasure and not pain. Therefore the Great Seal does not only aim to enlighten during meditation time but helps one to hold the pure view. Skillfully it encompasses all aspects of life and continues mind's experience of its potential through the day. Even during deep absorption the experiencer does not need to do anything wild to counteract the flow of inner events. Whoever jots down two words when something important pops up and continues meditating with the feeling of not having interrupted anything, enjoys freedom in abundance. The goal of the Diamond Way is to never leave the pure land and to separate meditation and the time between or after meditation as little as possible. This means to be aware of the perfect potential of beings and situations as well as one can between one's bouts of practice. Formerly Western cultures called this "being in the world but not of the world" and if psychedelic drugs were not harmful and their effects often lasting, then we might have created a generation like that in the sixties. The trick is to see the highest possibilities in whatever occurs. One then skillfully works with the available facts without letting them wear one down. Mature living is like staying in a hotel: One uses everything freely but is also aware that ultimately one can only bring one's impressions along in the end.

"In its non-artificial and natural state."

In the state of limitless freedom, everything is fearlessly enjoyed. "One may fearlessly enjoy," as Karma Pakshi, the second Karmapa said, "because everything is nothing anywhere but indestructible and spontaneously perfect mind." One's growing experience that whatever happens has to do with oneself, will create responsibility and compassion in all situations of life. It develops everybody's countless and inherent qualities, right here and now.

According to Buddha's Diamond Way, mind's finest capacities like intuition, fearlessness, self-arisen joy, and intelligent far-sighted love are neither foreign to us nor commandments imposed by gods or social patterns. They simply signify that mind recognizes itself. It is therefore noble to trust them and to recognize their power during the moments when few disturbances veil our awareness. Beyond expectation and anxiety and without the limitations of past or future, our objective must be the expression of its limitless abilities for the benefit of all. As nobody was ever enlightened yesterday or tomorrow but always right now, Buddha's highest teachings point to this non-artificial moment of truth where one recognizes the radiance behind and between experiences, that which knows and is aware.

As one's way to enlightenment means becoming independent, one's own ever-sharper conscience remains the ultimate judge. Our life is running well when we can calmly look into our eyes in the mirror because our motivation, words, and actions correspond. This is why one's natural growth through Buddha's teaching is so different from the commandments and rigid contracts of faith-religions. He allows his students a vast but critical gray zone for things to mature and gives the space for outer, inner, and secret levels of practice to complement each other. Fluently and at one's own discretion there is constant development.

"Skilled in sustaining this practice of mind's nature."

From the level of the Great Seal, this means never losing one's center and not judging oneself because of constantly changing thoughts. Instead, one remains in constant freshness, in the timeless play of space. Mind's habits are strong, however, and every hopeful practitioner will need a great deal of time to bravely learn to keep frustrations at bay. One must become aware of their impermanent nature and learn to compare one's own situation to those who really suffer like the poor in overpopulated countries or women under Islam. This leads to thicker skin and a more compassionate and outgoing style. Finally, even major difficulties will simply become a challenge, somehow exciting and new. At this point the thread of awareness is not lost even in the heat of the moment and one is at home in whatever happens.

Staying conscious during excitement, danger, and love as well as in one's daily life requires true perseverance. Whoever manages to keep one's space-awareness conscious also during intense experiences will make even the most trivial habits and doubts into milestones on his way to enlightenment and everything in life will gradually make sense. Nothing is more encouraging than conquering such hindrances. This is also true for observers who will then dare to try the same in their own lives.

1st Karmapa, Dusum Chenpa, 1110–93

ཕུ་རགས་རྟོག་པའི་དབའ་རླབས་རང་སར་ཞི། །

The waves of subtle and coarse thoughts are naturally calmed,

གཡོ་མེད་སེམས་ཀྱི་ཆུ་བོ་དང་གིས་གནས། །

and the waters of unshakable mind are settled.

ཞིང་རྨུགས་རྟོག་པའི་རྡི་མ་དང་བྲལ་བའི། །

May we rest in the smooth ocean of calm abiding,

ཞི་གནས་རྒྱ་མཚོ་མི་གཡོ་བརྟན་པར་ཤོག །

free of the blemish of inertia, dullness, and cloudiness.

VERSE 16

After the highest view of the Great Seal in so many verses, what follows here is less exciting but readily understandable, also from a conceptual level. In these four lines the 3rd Karmapa comments on the holding and calming types of meditation that are also known in other forms of religion. In Sanskrit, this state of absorption is called *shamatha* and hopefully leads to the penetrating insight called *vipashyana*. Tibetans use the terms *shi'ne* and *lhgtong*.

It seems reasonable to comment on this verse from an historical point of view. The period of the 3rd Karmapa (1284–1339) contained all the political influences that came up countless times over the centuries in the medieval society that was Tibet. This might explain the presence of this verse on calming mind in the middle of a teaching on mind's ultimate essence. As stories of the Kagyu lineage back to the times in India show, a teacher's Great Seal accomplishment could be transmitted at an early stage to those students who had obtained a certain state of openness or where a close connection existed from former lives. This was of course old news to the accomplishers living freely in the caves but also Gampopa, the first monk in the Kagyu lineage and the main teacher of the first Karmapa, dared to go against the common monastic grain and said that beyond the step by step ascent of the much-praised gradual paths, some students with a close bond to their lamas would be able to develop much more quickly. Because of devotion, courage, and an absence of clinging to fixed ideas, they would be able to very skillfully and directly absorb the qualities and activities of their teachers. Since the time of the 5th Karmapa (1384–1450), the pinnacle of such a transmission in the Karma Kagyu lineage has been the showing of the Black Crown by the Karmapas. Other earlier methods, used by lay accomplishers like Marpa and Milarepa to strongly bless or otherwise awaken their students, would certainly also have invoked the jealousy of many monastic teachers who work on the levels of morality and concepts and express little or no practical confidence in space. When such feelings came up, the Karmapas were aware of their concerns and tended to be more kind than insistent or competitive. They therefore withdrew or watered down their highest teachings for a while. For example in the thirteenth century, doubts expressed by the Sakya Pandita about certain rapid teaching techniques made the early Kagyu schools tone down their style; and though most Westerners would not compromise on something as important as that, it is a very Asian way of avoiding public trouble in areas that only few could access anyway. After all, one does not discuss a rainbow with someone who is color-blind or share the views of the Great Seal in a bad atmosphere.

The effectiveness of different viewpoints and approaches to realization in the world is still dependent upon the availability of good people to work with them. The wild accomplishers, who once lived in the caves but are now more often found parachuting, on motorcycles, surfing or with their friends at a bar, the learned people with their intellectual fulfillments and the virtuous monks or students living in the discipline of a monastery, will naturally find separate ways. It is a great richness that Buddha had the time to supply skillful means to all kinds of people

During the time of the Thirty-year War in Europe, in the first half of the seventeenth century and during the time of the

10th Karmapa, this jealousy between the lineages—because of the level of their teachings—increased even further. Also during about thirty years, the old schools of Tibetan Buddhism were ransacked by Mongolian soldiers invited by the 5th Dalai Lama. To be able to survive this, the Kagyus had to restrict the tantric or totally transforming teachings discussed here; and, instead, the sutras, a conceptual teaching, became the official basis for their practice. Several times the Kagyus handled criticism from their competitors by stressing the Great Way (Mahayana) teachings. They de-emphasized both the great richness of special Diamond Way methods as well as the highest view of the Great Seal—a transmission only they hold. To avoid further suppressions, the Kagyus then inserted the instructions on holding mind and obtaining insight (*shi-ne* and *lhgtong*), between the Four Foundational Practices and the teachings on the Great Seal.

As many Karmapas accurately foresaw the direction of future events, this verse can be understood to have the undertone of cooling people's tempers and avoiding attacks. But this does not make it boring. In Buddha's teachings, every development has the taste of liberation; and even the impermanence of all phenomena will look interesting in the right light. Karmapa here uses the example of the return of subtle and coarse inner states to space to express his own viewpoint of the Great Seal. He abides consciously in the aware radiance that lies between and behind the relative, which knows the essence of all mind's perceptions, feelings, and thoughts and therefore experiences these processes as self-liberating. Seen from this ultimate point of view, mind is both the power of awareness and whatever takes place; and nothing can diminish its freedom and space. His words bring relief on every mental level, but what frees beings most is that here a sustained development progresses under its own steam. Going beyond moralism and other unhealthy mental states, it is nourished by whatever does or does not happen. Unadjusted and left undisturbed, mind naturally relaxes through its own power. Holding the absolute view, neither grasping nor avoiding can change truth. From the moment the experiencer is conscious of his own true essence, fearlessness, joy, and love appear spontaneously as its true qualities. Actually, it is quite simple: seeing whatever happens as cause and effect or Karma, and understanding one's own as well as other beings' reactions to events as expressions of maturity, what can one do but develop through life?

In this verse, Karmapa once again chooses water for the artistic representation of his view. Through its flowing and basically pure qualities, he clarifies how mind works. When the waves of superficial impressions run out, mind neither loses consciousness and energy, nor simply becomes stale. Instead, it rests unshakably in its essence, recognizing itself to be both the ocean and its potential for waves. The fearlessness, continuous elation, and active compassion arising from this experience are not only absolute—having no other source than mind's space, awareness, and limitless nature—but they are also the noblest of feelings. Whoever possesses this certainty already has everything.

In Great Seal texts, beings' ordinary, changing inner states are compared to images in a mirror. In essence they are constantly fresh but do not last very long. This is why during one's development, mind's awareness gradually shifts away from impermanent phenomena and experiences more and more the timeless space its consciousness truly is. This is not a passive state, however; the realization of mind's boundless expression means action. Not separating doer, object, and thing done, one brings the conditions for peace and enriches, fascinates, and protects beings in lasting ways. During one's stages of development, where mind still employs concepts to check its progress, it joyfully notices a growing capacity for compassion. Sometimes, an apprehensive thought like: "Will I be tough enough for the challenges of life?" might come up; but in fact one just has less stiffness, expectations, or fear than before. In parallel, mirror-like, equalizing, discriminating, experiential, and all-pervading wisdoms spring up ever more easily and frequently. Increasingly, one learns to see the world from the here and now of one's own center; and finally, mind's pure power of consciousness illuminates everything. The timeless space of potential can now no longer be lost. It is and knows everything and feels united with all.

Symbolized by the ocean, Karmapa invokes a mental state beyond **"inertia, dullness, or cloudiness."** Here mind knows its timeless essence, nature, and expression. **"In the smooth ocean of calm abiding,"** the experiencer, the object experienced, and the act of experiencing are more and more known as one.

In the self-fulfilling awareness of a gigantic "a-ha," all things are transparent; and one knows through every atom in one's body. Outer and inner worlds appear, play freely, and dissolve; and every cell feels 10,000 volts of unending bliss. Insight, power, courage, wisdom, and compassion complete their growth. Highest truth and joy cannot be separated; and from its very depth, consciousness works steadfastly for the benefit of all.

Being essentially unchanging space, mind simultaneously expresses a richness that appears together with the power to recognize both its absolute and relative aspects. It may know its non-material space-essence and simultaneously remain aware of the relative interplay of cause and effect. As enlightenment becomes more real, one increasingly and beyond any doubt experiences mind's timeless radiance to be more appealing than even the most exciting pictures it may manifest. The growth of this conviction brings the accomplisher to his indestructible center.

This is not a question of "either-or": the waves and the ocean complement and enrich each another. When mind has discovered its timeless aspect and has gradually shifted its consciousness there, everything in life becomes a gift. The goal is to simultaneously be the mirror and its images, the ocean and its waves, the timeless experiencer and its conditioned and impermanent impressions and perceptions. The playful, spontaneous effortlessness that springs from this state is timelessly perfect.

The increasingly long periods of bliss, where everything is simply perfect and one's hair stands on end with joy, are not brought about by beings' ordinary search for happiness. No dualistic wish for pleasant experiences or attempts to avoid pain can have any lasting effect. Whatever one harvests from seeking happiness outside one's mind is only artificial, no matter how diligently one strives. Every attempt to bring one's body and mind to lasting joy through conditioned impressions happens in vain.

In the state beyond expectation and fear, mind will recognize its radiant power. Whoever focuses on past or future, however, instead of remaining simply and unaffectedly in the here and now will experience little of their timeless perfections. The inertia, dullness, and cloudiness that Karmapa mentions here should certainly be dropped.

If mind was always limitless awareness and perfect in its essence, why coin a phrase for its transient weaknesses? Why does Karmapa deal here with topics that fit so poorly with the noble style of the rest of his wishes? Apart from the possible political motivation already suggested a reason could be responsibility and compassion for his students. His words toughen up those on the first steps of the way for both spiritual growth and ordinary life. His teaching advises them to stay aware of what their minds do and to find something useful in even the most uninspiring situations. As the mental veils described above produce both bad feelings and block beings' way to enlightenment, this activity also has an additional meaning: the disclosure and transformation of obstructive disturbing feelings that makes their energy useful to others.

In his previous verse, Karmapa mentioned the **"winds of ordinary life,"** which knock beings off their way. Subsequently, he wishes beings deep mental peace without dullness because feeling disturbed, sleepy, or agitated are the greatest hindrances to one's meditation, particularly on the formless way. Until people start meditating most have not yet discovered that they can change these fundamental tendencies of unenlightened minds.

If sleepiness clouds one's meditation, the energy level in one's body is too low. In this case it is excellent to meditate on light-colored buddha forms. Also coffee or tea should help or one may imagine being full of transparent but heavy oil. At heart-level in the center of one's body one then lets a bubble of air appear. One remains one-pointedly focused on it as it moves steadily upwards, leaves the top of one's head and disappears among some clouds. It may also sharpen one's mind to imagine looking through an opalescent point between one's eyebrows. These simple techniques draw up one's energies and can make one feel fresh again.

If disturbing feelings are strong and one cannot find peace, one's energy level is too high in the body. In that case the best thing to do is to meditate on buddha aspects of a darker color. It also helps to eat something heavy. Again, one may meditate being full of transparent, heavy oil. But this time in

the center of one's chest is a small black ball, which is naturally heavy. One focuses on it as it falls slowly down through
the body, lets it leave through one's anus and then follows it
as it passes through the earth's crust and is lost somewhere
in its molten core. One may also simply concentrate on a
black point four hands in front of one's noble parts. These
approaches lower the energy and can settle mind.

In the **"ocean of calm abiding"** of the Great Seal teachings, every event becomes a friend and all things are gifts.
Mind discovers with constant amazement and bliss that in
spite of not being a thing, it is clearly not nothing. It is neither a black hole in which nothing happens nor a white wall
that only shows what is projected upon it. Instead, the limitless richness of complete awareness reveals the insights that
Karmapa shares in these verses for enlightenment. Behind
any changing experience there is always the clear light of
awareness that makes everything possible.

3rd Karmapa, Rangjung, 1284–1339

བསྐྱར་མའི་སེམས་ལ་ཡང་ཡང་བལྟས་པའི་ཚེ།

If we recurrently watch non-visible mind,

མཐོང་མེད་དོན་ནི་ཇི་བཞིན་ལྷག་གེར་མཐོང་།

its non-visible essence is known clearly and exactly as it is.

ཡིན་མིན་དོན་ལ་བྱེ་ཚོམ་ཆོད་པ་ཉིད།

This severs all doubts about mind's being or non-being.

འཁྲུལ་མེད་རང་ངོ་རང་གིས་ཤེས་པར་ཤོག།

May its undeluded essence recognize itself.

VERSE 17

In this verse Karmapa again touches upon the limits of what can be communicated with words. Whoever follows him and does not begrudge himself the freedom of conceptless space that these teachings lay open, will have great joy. That is the nature of the Great Seal. Mind cannot be found because it is not a thing. No part of it can be made visible or examined. As it is without size, weight, or color, without middle and in every way empty of anything limiting, it also cannot observe itself from somewhere else. What sees and what is seen—both are mind.

Whoever realizes this and therefore stops trying to prove any object to be separate from its experiencer will enjoy increasing periods of mind's intuitive insight. This will gradually liberate its other inherent buddha qualities, and mind will experience its totality for ever-longer periods. Ultimately its radiant essence will pervade everything and knows no limits in time. This identification with what is aware, the constant feeling of oneness between that which sees and that which appears, is the goal, the Great Seal. It brings forth a state where any experience is recognized as being mind's free play, joyful and rich, simply because it can take place.

The practices of the Diamond Way accomplishers open the direct way to this enlightening and highest view. One will recognize in brief glimpses and also come to accept from teachers with real life experience that this world is a pure land and that only one's mental veils keep one from that realization. Therefore one must consciously strive to obtain the highest level of insight and get the best out of every situation. Because of one's understanding of highest truth being highest joy, this never becomes a way to dodge life's confrontations; it is also not the creation of some sweet and fuzzy dream. One now handles life effectively on a practical level, while at the same time knowing that absolute time-less truth is even more wonderful than the finest dream and that one is therefore right to behave like a buddha until one becomes one. The state to be obtained is that of a child who accidentally opens the door to a vast, gleaming hall and can only say "Wow." This original freshness in every moment must not be lost in the wear and tear of everyday life, but should find nourishment in every experience and experience made and strengthen itself for the benefit of others. On the relative level, one needs a toolbox for handling the world and being useful in one's environment, but maturity means not to hold it in front of one's eyes as it will block one's view. Instead one keeps it to the side so that one can freely use the hammers and saws as necessary and fully enjoys the richness of what boundless space brings forth and has the power to experience.

This power of consciousness is mind's light. It consists of a non-ceasing flow of fresh "a-ha" experiences and there exists no other enlightened experience than knowing that. Although enlightenment's self-arisen bliss transforms one totally and makes one's heart too big for one's rib–cage, it is nothing but one's own mind.

On one's way to this timeless and ever-new happiness, doubts about mind's being or non-being disappear. One's understanding of the mental essence and interdependency of the world and consciousness becomes complete certainty. Manifestation and mind are one from then on. One lives in a state of full satisfaction, right here and now. Beyond any expectation or fear, one handles every challenge as it appears and with good conscience. One knows that it is in accordance with the most far-sighted solution for beings' greatest development. The key to this level of functioning is a perception free of mental veils. Its view of absolute purity dissolves any disturbances. With fascination one recognizes evermore how the world appears as the collective dream of beings, but also that it has enough elasticity for the strong Karmas of individuals or groups to change it—that the influence of blessings, wishes, and one-pointed meditations remain active until the full development of impressions have brought a result. Whereas karma is not fate, tendencies and influences can derail whole chains of causes and effects. Actually it is sad that people so frequently destroy the enjoyment of this cosmic circus through their changing moods. If they could experience the uniqueness of their situations, every drama would instead be a celebration.

Free, easy, and rich in methods, the holder of the Great Seal recognizes beings' wish for happiness. Sharing the passing joys on the way, he guides them to become aware of mind, their only source. Abiding in one's center, one notices with thankfulness how this disposition makes everything mature at the right time and place and for the lasting benefit of beings. Thus one learns to trust the basic goodness of mind's potential and acts from the experience of oneness with body, speech, and mind. Nothing shows the potential of space better than the accomplishment of successful deeds.

ཕྱལ་ལ་བལྟས་པས་ཕྱལ་མེད་སེམས་སུ་མཐོང་།

Observing phenomena, none is found. One sees mind.

སེམས་ལ་བལྟས་པས་སེམས་མེད་ངོ་བོས་སྟོང་།

Looking at mind, no mind is seen, it is empty in essence.

གཉིས་ལ་བལྟས་པས་གཉིས་འཛིན་རང་སར་གྲོལ།

Through looking at both, one's clinging to duality
naturally dissolves.

འོད་གསལ་སེམས་ཀྱི་གནས་ལུགས་རྟོགས་པར་ཤོག།

May we realize mind's nature, which is clear light.

VERSE 18

A verse of this kind produces bliss in every accomplisher. In its few words Karmapa transmits a complete and enlightened view. Whoever understands this needs nothing else on his way. Yet, a great deal of focused work and confidence in mind are needed to go from the enjoyment of his clear words to absolute certainty. Only fresh minds with a great deal of space and a basically happy disposition can manage such a process.

And what is the message here? In all modesty his words establish everything outer and inner to be mind, and he states that mind is essentially space. They expose all duality as being ultimately false and untangles the basic questions of countless philosophers over thousands of years. Karmapa manages to achieve this without having to prove or deny anything. He simply examines the nature of things in the light of the teachings that Buddha gave his closest friends two thousand five hundred and fifty years ago. A detailed examination of phenomena shows that they do not exist independently and that they have no lasting nature. This does not only relate to one's own perception, which clearly appears, changes, and disappears; but it is equally valid, although less easily noticed, for the outer world, which one shares with others.

The objects of one's awareness, which are usually felt to be so real, are actually a never-ending stream of circumstances. Buddha captured this in the memorable phrase: "Form is emptiness." This is, however, only a partial insight that should not lead to nihilism. Empty spaces, be they in one's consciousness or in laboratories, tend to fill themselves up (as shown in Stanford University's physics experiments). Therefore, in the same breath Buddha continues: "Emptiness is form." By now one should realize that this does not validate materialism. Finally, with his third statement, "Form and emptiness are inseparable," he ensures the freedom of those students who have just kicked out their two strongest mental patterns from adopting another intellectually based or otherwise limiting view. The three teachings together are his key to mind's great expanse and its free play.

Actually, someone's realization of this wisdom is only perfect when he can turn himself into a rainbow at will. While Karmapa's simple but logical words completely contradict beings' sensory input and day-to-day experiences, at the same time they bring the Karma-structures, which chain unenlightened beings to their habitual world, into a relative light.

Many would probably appreciate a gradual, practical, and understandable approach to this rendition of absolute truth. Only in a state of deep absorption, where all mind's facets have been activated, can such absolute statements be truly realized. Mind also cannot be grasped, for it is "empty" of any characteristics. To conquer such obstacles to non-dual and intuitive perception, students on the Diamond Way must jump ever further into space, with complete confidence. Whoever manages this ultimate fusion of subject, object, and action, needs nothing more for happiness. Accomplishing the pure view and being at home in the clear light that experiences and rests timelessly inside, between, and behind mental activity, one will be showered with gifts.

Outer and inner events are mind's abundance and potential; and if one examines them thoroughly, only the experiencer remains. Although one may habitually expect at least this to be a "something," one is left with just space. Actually, this discovery is a boundless, joyful experience that allows everything to happen. The separation between experiencer and object experienced falls away, and one can truly relax. The first steps of this realization process already sweep masses of obstacles from the realm of the practitioner's habitual feelings. However, they only release the hammerlock on the mind hosting them when the illusion of a separate "I" fully disintegrates. Until then, one considers the changing inner states to be more or less real and permits them to color one's view, giving them varying amounts of influence over one's body and speech.

Everybody knows that, when pleasant impressions ripen from one's store-consciousness and one feels good, one's world is experienced as pleasant and attractive and one behaves accordingly. This may take place at times when the people around one experience the very opposite and it shows how strong subjectivity is. The same happens when indigestible impressions surface. One sees faults and hindrances everywhere and becomes frustrated. Both of these tendencies plant seeds for the future. In addition to this, the natural limits of one's sensory organs, cultural background, former experiences, and style of education determine one's field of awareness.

The underlying reason for this is the variation in people's karmas. It explains why praiseworthy attempts at integration around the world generally do not succeed and why personal relationships between people with considerably different backgrounds often end dramatically. Studies now show that their children often cannot find a secure basis in either parent's culture and subsequently suffer.

So those are some details about the experiencer. What is experienced is equally exciting. The collective dream or the outer world of the senses that condenses from the limitless potential of space and the karmas of countless beings is also nothing but mind and is therefore essentially space. In this verse, Karmapa intensively works the realm of fundamental truths. He describes the emptiness and conditioned nature of everything inner and outer and shows every dualistic experience to be an illusion. In what way, then, does free and all-pervading space manifest? As **"clear light"** and highest joy! One needs neither to die to inhabit a pure land nor to go somewhere else to meet buddhas; perfecting one's view is enough. What one needs is a readiness to see evermore clearly what really is supported by the intelligent determination to remove the veils of disturbing feelings and ignorance from mind. Soon the realization dawns that everything has ultimate meaning simply because it happens or doesn't happen and that every thought is wisdom simply because it can appear. With the deepest of thankfulness, one realizes that every particle vibrates with happiness and is kept together by love.

For enlightened beings, the world is not the condensation of five disturbing feelings but the expression of five wisdoms. They experience pure realms always and everywhere and see the power-circles of radiant buddhas in each atom. Everything is then meaningful, true, and exciting, because it shows mind's capacity through all that happens. Where anger might have appeared from a dualistic point of view, enlightened beings experience a radiant wisdom, which reflects everything like a mirror. Instead of feeling superior with the kind of pride that turns others into miserable company, they see mind's play and its rich potential in whatever appears. Attachment becomes the ability to discriminate, understanding phenomena both singly and in their wider context. What might have become jealousy can now cut through situations clearly. One recognizes the sequence of events through past, present, and future. During this process insights are naturally accumulated, and one develops the power to act in a beyond-personal way. Above all else, intuition reigns supreme. Supported by these four wisdoms, events, confusion, and ignorance manifest as all-pervading insight. Where one has the most waste, one can produce the best compost; and on the Diamond Way one's biggest problem becomes one's best friend. Here anger makes one like a diamond, shining and indestructible. Pride produces a jewel-like appearance, naturally rich and radiant. Desire transforms into the lotus-like qualities of nourishing and caring; jealousy makes one like a sword, able to cut through and separate what doesn't belong together; and as the clouds of ignorance empty of rain, stupidity becomes the buddha state.

From the level of liberation, where one's belief in a real and existent "I" disappears, one experiences suffering as obtaining a dream-like quality that is no longer binding. During one's further development, the extent to which one experiences pure realms of consciousness increases; and one has a growing awareness that all beings are buddhas who have not yet recognized their essence. Whatever happens on these levels expresses the peace-giving, increasing, fascinating, and protective buddha activities, where everything is rich and self-liberating. Although no separate seer can be established, much is seen. Getting the seer to see himself is Buddha's enlightening gift.

"Through looking at both, one's clinging to duality naturally dissolves."

It is understandable that even many highly intelligent people can draw little actual joy or practical benefit from self-explanatory statements like those above. Without a close connection to a strong teacher who embodies such experiences, they simply do not dare to trust space. Instead, many turn to difficult, patronizing, and creating gods. They refuse to be critical or laugh when practices or people are funny. They also claim that some "subtle material"—however they may imagine that to be—is the cause of outer phenomena. Although such explanations may be much closer to a world where most beings feel comfortable than to Buddha's insistence on the ultimate emptiness of everything, such "apparent" solutions cause their adherents constant difficulties. If one follows their logic, their personal gods must be conditioned and therefore impermanent. If gods are here and not there, they cannot be one with everything. What has borders towards the outside will be composite towards the inside. The gods must therefore have been put together, created, or born. This means that due to their conditioned nature, they must also one day fall apart, die, or disappear. In this way, either everything is true or nothing is; but by observing cause and effect at work, it is reasonable to decide that all is true, whether being's personal universes can absorb that insight or not. Additionally, any personal "self" that is aware of these gods must share these limitations in time and space. The insight necessary for true fearlessness, as well as for discovering one's unshakable center, is that mind is nothing substantial that will fall apart, but timeless space. This is why beings' essence is indestructible. What is aware, is in essence, one with everything, whether this is experienced or not, and all beings are buddhas surrounded by other buddhas emanating spontaneous powerfields of highest bliss.

Yogi Chen was a Chinese accomplisher who became known through scores of most interesting, juicy, and frequently controversial booklets about Buddhism, frequently comparing its logic to the weaknesses of other religions. After fleeing the communists who destroyed his family, he spent twenty-seven years in the same house in Kalimpong, never going more than seven steps from his front door. Hannah and I knew him well in the early 1970s and he expressed his understanding like this: "No mind, no worry." Sometimes he also said: "If mind cannot be found, nobody needs to fear that it could disappear or die."

Holding the highest view, no matter how far it may be from the relative world of experience, does not make beings spacey or bring about misguided actions. As ever-deeper wisdom permeates body and speech, every action becomes effortless and is in tune with each situation. Even while heavy karmas still surface, such a disposition wards off many unpleasant experiences or transforms them into maturity and benefit for others. In this greatest of blessing-fields, which is truth-space itself, everything arises at the right juncture. Neither too early nor too late, the conditions for maximal growth will appear. Having established such certainty, nothing else is needed. Events then become an expression of basic richness and are free and playful in themselves. Instead of freezing in an unexpected situation like a bull who returns to find the barn door closed, one now sees the potential in the situation. Thinking, "there may be another door at back of the building" or "maybe I should just stay out anyway and meet a cow" or "I can flatten that stupid barn," one works from the freedom of space.

This is also the way to understand Karmapa's statement: **"Through looking at both, one's clinging to duality naturally dissolves."** It shows that whoever explores both the outer world and one's own mind will recognize the essence of both to be neither a thing nor just empty space. One will thus stop separating experiencer, object experienced, and the act of experiencing. Any true insight gained into mind and the world unites the seer, what is seen, and the process of seeing itself. The way all phenomena are mutually dependent and in a state of flux, they are also empty of any lasting characteristics. Except for potential or space, nothing has permanence either inside or out. Instead, beings' general tendencies condense into the jointly experienced outer world, while their personal karma colors their place in and perception of it. Both unfold in space, are recognized through its clarity, and return to its boundlessness. Whoever searches for either the experiencer or the experience will find openness and nothing else. This realization changes everything. Separations between oneself and others, between the inner and outer worlds, and between being and non-being here become the unfolding of a totality. At the same time one's mind is seen to be the indestructible player and observer of it all. The realization that there is no ultimate nothingness that one may get lost in—because "experiencing space," its awareness and its limitless expressions are in the end one—frees mind's fresh and creative joy.

Almost every population has cultural bottlenecks that hinder the realization of freedom and happiness by its members. In the case of the modern Westerner, who otherwise enjoys the best of education and freedom, a main problem continues to be uncertainty about the interaction of brain and mind. This produces much unnecessary anxiety, but it does not need to be this way.

If, as a materialistic world today presupposes, brain would actually produce mind, then both would be impermanent. In this case, the creation of a better world for future generations would still have some meaning, but many busy people would probably think that those who work with their own development in this life are wasting their time. They would instead settle for simply enjoying whatever is possible, here and now, which is what most people generally do anyway. This view of the world and its life forms may at first glance seem quite comfortable, but it is surely not satisfactory. This can be seen from the empty expression in the eyes of so many materially well-endowed people. If mind would disappear with the destruction of one's brain, nothing would continue or give timeless meaning to life.

At the end of the last World War the forces of materialism and communism looked exceedingly powerful, and many in the free West felt they would need to control their societies along similar lines for protection. We are all most lucky that at this point the unquestionably good karmas and massive thirst for liberty of the mind-expanding generation of the sixties ensured today's freedom. They created those vast chemical cracks in the fortress of materialistic thinking that are today bringing Buddhism and science ever closer together. Not to mention the humanistic disciplines like psychology and philosophy, where the influence was to be expected. Buddhism has proven a useful frame for evaluating precise experiments into the behavior of the smallest particles as well as for an understanding of the cosmos.

The discoveries on the cutting edge of science at the beginning of the third millennium become evermore Buddhist. It seems that whether one looks inside through meditation or checks the outer scene with today's research equipment, the same world is seen. In any case, to those who follow events, the great nihilistic scare that the world is a meaningless machine and that space is just a black hole seems increasingly groundless. Concerning mind, more observations are explained if one postulates that it is transformed by the brain than if it were being produced by it. Whoever takes a moment to compare the number of people they know who could telephone or write with how often they intuitively know exactly who is calling or how frequently they think strongly of somebody and then discover that their letter was already in the mail, will see that space is information and will surely feel connected. They will not consider their surrounding medium something that is separating or dead but instead notice that it is a container that both holds and gives meaning to all. Seeing the brain as the receiver and not the transmitter makes sense. Mind is then understood to be a beginningless stream of conditioned impressions, which moves through countless bodies. From life to life, it expresses its content while also creating the new impressions that will mature into its next existence.

Whoever does not recognize mind's timeless aspect will identify with the flow of changing moments and lives to which they have attached themselves. This beginningless play, where even the highest joy is less than the constant bliss of enlightenment, will continue until mind's timeless radiance is known. Through dissolving fixed concepts, like those of being and non-being, and accompanied by the growing understanding that the experienced duality of a "you" and a "me" is illusory, everything forced falls away by itself. This leads to the full flowering of mind's wisdom, joy and its historically conscious compassion.

With this verse, Karmapa freed the mole of habitual mind from its tunnels. He exchanged the narrow view of "either-or" with the vast, beyond-dualistic "both-and" of Buddhism. With contact lenses on its eyes, wings tied to its paws, and feathers on its tail, Karmapa sets mind free to soar into the sky like an eagle.

8th Karmapa, Mikyo Dorje, 1507–54

ཡིད་བྱེད་བྲལ་བ་འདི་ནི་ཕྱག་རྒྱ་ཆེ།

Free from mental fabrication, it is the state of the Great Seal
(Maha-mudra).

མཐའ་དང་བྲལ་བ་དབུ་མ་ཆེན་པོ་ཡིན།

Free of extremes, it is the Great Middle Way (Maha-madhyamaka).

འདི་ནི་ཀུན་འདུས་རྫོགས་ཆེན་ཞེས་ཀྱང་བྱ།

All encompassing, it is also called the Great Perfection (Maha-ati).

གཅིག་ཤེས་ཀུན་དོན་རྟོགས་པའི་གདེངས་ཐོབ་ཤོག།

By knowing one, may we attain conviction in the realization of all.

VERSE 19

With this verse Karmapa continues to cruise at maximum altitude, abiding completely in the vastness of mind. Here he gives an overview of two of the three view-transforming or tantric transmissions, those of the Nyingma or Old School and of the Kagyu or Oral Transmission. He may have considered the Sakya tradition (the third of these early "Red Hat" schools, named after a region in Tibet) too critical of widely sharing such high teachings and thus did not include them in this text. However, he does include the highest intellectual and motivation-transforming teachings of what is now the "Yellow Hat" Tibetan school of the Virtuous Ones, the Gelugpas of the Dalai Lamas. They are mainly monastic and appeared later when a student of the 4th Karmapa became the teacher of the first Dalai Lama. At the time of this text, many of their teachings were in the hands of a school called the Khadampas.

As would be expected from an accomplisher, Karmapa only needs a few words to give the full picture. He transmits the taste of the highest teachings of these three schools; and whoever is in the know will laugh up their sleeves. One can still recognize the unchanged character of these transmissions today. Their vibrations and distinctive tendencies followed 85,000 Tibetan escapees across the Himalayas to India in 1959; and twelve years later those same energies started traveling on to the West, with some inspired hippies and the lamas of the different lineages. Karmapa's testimony concerning the different ways thus remains totally contemporary, seven hundred years later. Basic human traits don't change, teachers attract their own kind, and the sentiments that his words describe are still meaningful today. Therefore the comparisons made in this verse and their interpretations feed frequent discussions between the schools of Tibetan Buddhism. Even to the most politically correct and overly conscientious representatives of that toothless kind of equanimity that tries to avoid any objective or discriminating reasoning in order to keep things sweet, these words are seeded with landmines and awaken the most turbulent of emotions.

Every enlightened realization is inherent in mind, which is and encompasses everything. They are its timeless essence. The teaching that all things are made possible by and happen in mind and that it knows everything, cannot be kept apart from anything, and contains all phenomena in its limitless awareness—this teaching is an open invitation for all. Beings find their way to this ultimate realization through different methods and at varying speeds. Therefore Buddha taught according to their capacity, giving three ways and 84,000 methods for liberation and enlightenment.

Historically, whoever wanted to recognize mind quickly and directly through its space-awareness headed for the methods of the Diamond Way. The general feeling today is that the Buddhas invite those who come. Still, one should check any hopeful candidates whenever possible so nobody wastes their time in the wrong religion or on the wrong level of Buddha's teaching: Is there a basic foundation of compassion and wisdom? Are courage, confidence, and self-sustaining enthusiasm present? And will he or she be able to progressively give up pride? If the answers to these questions are in the affirmative, he or she would probably benefit from the teachings and could be given responsibility in the group. After completing the Four Foundational Practices or Ngondro, which most effectively prepare body, speech, and mind, one would be shown further steps. Ultimately with more or less intermediary practices, they would enable mind to recognize itself through its awareness, its energy, or its ability to identify with representations of enlightenment. This was the approach of the three old transmissions that existed during the time of the 3rd Karmapa and their blessing is overwhelming. The views of the "Great Seal" and "Great Perfection" teachings go to one's core and are experienced on one's innermost level. They are self-liberating and touch the practitioner's totality. Activating one's qualities, activity, idealism, courage, and joy in a lasting way, they are truly magnificent gifts.

If a student was less wild but rather more inclined towards study, wishing to develop wisdom and compassion from a secure basis, then a different route might be used. The conceptual means of the Great Way (Mahayana) would be employed and in the Kagyu school he would first study the *Jewel Ornament of Liberation*[1] or today *The Way Things Are*,[2] before moving on as guided by his teacher.

Though they probably spent their youth rebelling against it, those with a lasting interest in the ultimate teachings of the Diamond Way will have a foundation from former lives concerning reasonable behavior and a rich inner life. This makes these levels of teachings into old friends and after the necessary years of proving one's strength one is glad to meet with them again. Still, one should not be afraid to use them as steps and instead go for the highest level that one can realistically practice. Life is short, some may need exactly what we have to offer, and every new body takes many years to train. Honestly and frequently one should therefore ask oneself:

1. Gampopa, *The Jewel Ornament of Liberation*. (Berkeley CA: Parallax Press, 1994).
2. Lama Ole Nydahl, *The Way Things Are*. (Nevada City, CA: Blue Dolphin, 1996; Winchester, UK: O Books, 2008).

"Am I really using this life? Am I doing my best? Do I think of others and mostly hold a beyond-personal view?" Above all else, if one can comfortably affirm that one increasingly experiences the freshness and free play of many situations, then one is receiving the right teachings and is at the right time and place.

People's knowledge of the general structure of Buddha's ways, the Western names of the buddha forms, and our own terms for the tools of inner growth will have to become commonplace. Though Buddha himself spoke a language somewhere between Sanskrit and Pali, the reason his teachings can flourish and bring an amazing level of mental health to many people worldwide is purely because they were translated. Otherwise such wisdom may disappear into museums as an exotic spiritual import or hide away in monasteries at a great distance from people's actual lives. Nine hundred and fifty years ago the hero Marpa translated into Tibetan those teachings given in India sixteen hundred years before his time and they have benefited countless beings up until today. Only the mantras, which have a deeper effect due to their vibration and transmission than through their meaning, are always kept as close as possible to one's teacher's—a point that sometimes has funny side effects. Most Western Kagyus today say the mantras that invoke the buddha aspects in the fearsome East Tibetan dialect of Kham, a Kagyu stronghold. The people there protected the country and every man was a king. They were also the robbers and warriors from whom our teacher, the 16th Karmapa, came. Many Gelugpas on the other hand invoke them in the cultured language of Lhasa bureaucrats. Luckily, the Buddhas understand all accents.

Evermore conscious and educated people, however, now wish to practice on the formless level of ultimate view. Therefore what was called *Maha-mudra, Maha-madhyamaka* and *Maha-ati* in India and became *Chag Chen, Uma Chenpo,* and *Dzog Chen* in Tibetan, today benefit the brightest of minds under the names of the Great Seal, Great Middle Way and Great Perfection. They are a boundless gift, celebrating both mind's power of fascination and its potential for awareness.

How could one's path to such treasures look? Well, one way is broad and safe. When one's relationship with the outer world has relaxed after employing Buddha's classic teachings on cause and effect that relate to one's situation, one's inner life will naturally arise. This opens mind to worlds of compassion and wisdom. When its conceptual peak has been reached, through the highly elaborate and beyond-dualistic view of the Great Middle Way, mind's confidence in its indestructible essence awakes in many. One may now securely and from a broad basis of understanding try one's appetite for the Diamond Way and its view of the Great Seal. Like skydivers jumping joyfully from airplanes knowing that modern parachutes work, one here embraces the perfection of space and all that it is.

The deeply transformative methods employed in the tantras and all-encompassing tools of the Great Seal and the Great Perfection bring about a rapid absorption of Buddha's qualities, which should—if at all possible—be exemplified by one's teacher. Vast potential, full of possibilities, is here generated through the phase of completion, where one melts together with the Buddhas or one's teacher and becomes space and awareness inseparable. This state will eventually extend into full enlightenment; so nothing is more precious. Such complete methods remain active as long as one trusts one's ultimate nature and keeps the bonds to one's lama. Also when one's ego is in the process of taking heavy blows, one should fight to keep the highest view with all one can muster and never let it slip away. On the level of understanding, the support required is to never forget that highest truth is highest joy. Whenever possible, one should take refuge for immediate strength and consciously decide to never leave one's "Pure Land." While the lama adds further dimensions of inner and secret reassurance, one should do one's best to ensure that one is not disturbed by any negativity that may manifest. The important thing to remember is that one is on one's way. Mind's impressions were stored during the countless situations of innumerable lives. It is therefore very understandable that attachment, confusion, and aversion do not disappear at once. Actually one may see everything pleasant as a blessing while everything unpleasant is a purification and therefore also useful. While difficult feelings will become less important, connections made to a Diamond Way teacher's energy field, his or her style of living and teaching, and the predominance of one of these three feelings in the student will determine which of the these three ways will be most useful. These conditions decide which approach can best activate the most of one's inherent enlightened potential.

"Free from mental fabrication, it is the state of the Great Seal."

In the Kagyu lineages a thankful confidence in one's lama and his transmission, combined with a predominance of desire is the disposition that indicates one's affinity for the rich approaches of the lay person and accomplisher. The main philosophical term for the goal here is *detong,* from *dewa* (bliss) and *tongpa* (space) meaning that these qualities are inseparable in true enlightenment. This can be clearly felt as fun and freedom when things flow naturally. In situations where Diamond Way bonds are broken, however, this same energy produces a suffocating atmosphere and such groups lose their relevance. This is understandable. In the Kagyu Oral Transmission, nothing functions without human warmth. Holders of the Great Seal are deeply enthralled with the potential in every situation, with the exciting qualities of beings, and the fact that anything can happen. This position contains a basic affirmation of life, and one is open to whatever seems fresh and new. What determines whether this view matures healthily into continually higher levels of development or turns into frustration, depends on two factors. The teacher needs to show a continuous and clear example, and the students must be willing to gradually shed many pre-conceived ideas. In particular for the lay people and accomplishers, one's relationship to the body and its sexuality should be relaxed, avoiding the suppressive moralistic attitudes of most religions. Treating one's mind like a beautiful garden where one would only plant the best of impressions, one remembers that one is basically always safe; indestructible awareness is more perfect than anything it can produce. One therefore chooses to notice what is exciting and pleasurable for others and oneself and to experience other beings and our shared world as attractive and fascinating. In an atmosphere like this, mind can easily bring forth its perfect beyond-personal qualities. The raw material of desire progresses through thankfulness and confidence and then on to devotion, enabling one to quickly absorb the qualities of the Buddhas and one's teachers. One is enabled to use this way by a willingness to evaluate even the strongest of experiences from a beyond-personal level. It can be endangered though, by excessive emotionalism, the tendency to waste important time expecting things and becoming dependent upon experiences.

If practitioners and groups don't dare to simply use such views in life as seems fit, they underestimate themselves to the detriment of many. Instead of taking on life's challenges themselves, they wait far too long for the next person who carries official blessing to come by. Misunderstood humility and a consumer attitude can easily block one's development, and older students should seek a healthy balance between being thankful for the greatness of one's teacher's gifts and trusting oneself to also pass on the aspects of them which one has realized.

For people whose desire and attachment is the predominant emotion, the Great Seal teachings of knowing mind through its joy are thus the most suitable way. It brings an enlightened view of events together with their complete experience. Returning to one of Karmapa's water analogies, it is as total and convincing as swimming or surfing in the ocean. Free of any limitations, it permits one to effortlessly abide in the here and now, making every experience wider and more meaningful. Above all, the tantric methods used involve body, speech, and mind and allow one to experience life's full variety. Everything has greatest meaning when the experiencer and all that it expresses, outwardly and inwardly, are inseparable and self-enriching.

"Free of extremes, it is the Great Middle Way."

Although less exciting than swimming, it is useful to establish essential facts about the ocean—for example by analyzing a water-sample. This meticulous approach, which is based on but then transcends concepts, is called the Great Middle Way. It is the continuation and crowning glory of the Great Way and works with the information contained in Buddha's sutras. The groups that use these teachings are often led by monks and nuns who may be Tibetan or Westerners and this seems to fit both the students and the subject matter. The

Great Middle Way is the general approach of the Gelugpa or Virtuous school, who have even developed a sutra *Mahamudra* where one reasons one's way through the steps of liberation and towards enlightenment. Remaining on the level of concept, thought, and analysis, however, this way and its realization of emptiness differs markedly from the tantric or total experience of the old or Red Hat lineages. The latter point to the essence of mind the very moment that awareness and confidence can be awakened and then give the students methods and blessing to perfect the total and pure view that they received. This brings practical and transforming experiences of identification with enlightenment to those who want and can handle them.

Buddha's sutric teachings are impartial, like something taught in a school. They are easy to categorize and allow thoughts of wisdom to seep from one's head to one's heart. This produces a secure and gradual development. Reaching full enlightenment in this way, however, is described as lasting three innumerable world cycles, which has brought many impatient students to inquire about the Diamond Way. One should consider this well however. Going from even the best motivation to a beyond-conceptual trust in the wide open potential of space is a huge jump. As already mentioned in these commentaries to the Great Seal, one may fall badly if one breaks one's bond or loses one's willingness to hold the pure view. On the other hand, however, one receives masses of help; and those same Diamond Way texts promise liberation and even enlightenment if basis, way, and goal all fit. The biographies of amazing accomplishers such as Guru Rinpoche, Marpa, Milarepa, and several Karmapas are impressive examples of this and still inspire people today.

Any discussion of quick or slow methods however, is completely futile and irrelevant. Knowing that life is short, everyone should seek the best methods for themselves with a minimum of pride and remember that any progress is individual. Whoever absorbs relevant teachings for oneself and later meditates upon the basis of a secure knowledge will be well equipped for one's way. Even those who can move forward quickly because of strong devotion from former lives still have to learn enough Buddhism to understand the beyond-personal framework of what is going on. Otherwise things again become tight, and they are unable to help others. Any contact with teachings about compassion and wisdom has a maturing effect; and although the highest level of identification may be quick and exciting, one does not have to be on it to develop!

The Great Middle Way is especially good for people who wish to develop consciously, gradually, and in accordance with any accepted morality. They are not mental parachutists or drivers of fast motorcycles, and their main disturbance is confusion. Their feelings are not very strong and they are often unsure of what they really want. As they are not fiery-tempered, this way of reflection and learning accords closely with their human style. Every well-grounded piece of information concerning mind must bring inner relaxation and thereby different kinds of wisdom and experience. Even though this method of accumulating the necessary conditions for recognizing mind is more complicated and time consuming, in the hands of trustworthy teachers, each of Buddha's ways brings one to the goal and has profound meaning.

"All encompassing, it is also called the Great Perfection."

The Great Perfection belongs to the tantras like the Great Seal. Using body, speech, and mind, it aims directly for absolute experience. This deep approach is used especially by the

Nyingma or Old School of Tibetan Buddhism, which prefers to use the name "Dzogchen in the West." Their observation of mind focuses on the return of outer as well as inner phenomena to space without anything having changed in its timeless essence. Its practitioners experience the experiencer through its self-liberating power. One is relieved to be again free of whatever occurred and expands one's awareness through realizing that mind liberates itself naturally from every impression.

While desire motivated the Great Seal and confusion the Great Middle Way, people with a tendency towards pride and anger are attracted to the Great Perfection, and this is evident today in the Western Dzogchen groups. While a meeting of Kagyus who practice the Great Seal may look like the annual convention of pickpockets with people holding and touching one another, and a gathering of the Gelugpas who study the Great Middle Way reminds one of a boarding school, the Nyingma groups consciously keep more distance between themselves and know in detail their position and what they don't like. Their source of development is above all the blessing of the great tantric master Guru Rinpoche, who established Buddhism in Tibet for the first time around AD 750. His power also permeates the Sakya and Kagyu lineages while many Gelugpas don't like him because he physically blessed so many women. The magnitude of his highest view is central to the Nyingma school. Returning to the earlier examples, in the Great Perfection one would come to know the essence of water by flying over the sea. It is known that since Buddha's time the holders of the Great Seal and the Great Perfection meditated together and that both transmissions were often held by the same lama. The 3rd Karmapa, who is said to have been the only holder of one transmission of the Great Perfection at his time, included its view and methods in the

Great Seal used today. Thus much of the essence is similar. Concerning terminology, however, one must genuinely watch out. The terms describing one's perception and steps on the way are often very different and thus misleading.

The Sakyapas, the third of the old tantric lineages, are not mentioned by Karmapa. They have particularly accurate and special initiations that they only give to very small groups and work with a conceptual and learned approach to the Great Seal. A high degree of their transmission takes place through family ties. After fleeing in 1959, they have established their main new seats in Singapore and Seattle. Their formless teachings are called Lam Drel and also have the strength to give a direct, beyond-conceptual experience of all mind's levels.

Although seven hundred years ago the Karmapa did not mention these meditations with form, I will add a few lines of information, for the sake of giving the complete picture of Diamond Way Buddhism today.

Mind's power to know, to act, and to be inspired can all be the mirror that shows its essence. As the teachings so far have focused on its awareness-aspects, here is a short overview of one's possible work on the levels of form and identification. Whoever is inspired to behave like a Buddha until he becomes one has found the fastest and most total of ways that even unites the methods for mind's ability to know and to act.

If dominant attachment brings one to the Great Seal, one will feel an affinity towards the peerless (Skt. *Anuttara*) level of the united buddha forms from the Mother tantras. Here, due to spontaneous confidence, one often requires only a short building-up phase during meditation. One instead relishes the chance to stay in radiant awareness for as long as possible during the completion phase of union with the

Buddhas. Here, an intelligent day-to-day motivation would be to stay aware of the impermanence of all phenomena while sharing any good experience consciously with others.

If because of insecurity one is attracted to the Great Middle Way, in Tibet one would not do meditations where one identifies with buddha forms until much later. As the famous Geshe Rabten and other lamas of Tibet's state church recount, in the enormous Gelugpa monasteries of Tibet this frequently meant waiting until one had first studied for twenty years. Today, however, the prevalent thirst for experience in the West and also among new groups in the East has shortened this process and now initiations are widely given, especially into the "non-dual" class of tantras like Kalachakra. It is very important, however, to find out what one will be promising before taking any initiations. With several of these teachers one may be about to agree to do hour-long practices every day!

The generally school-like atmosphere and the student's less direct bond to a teacher—together with the wide choice of possible instructions and explanations given—make many waver between experiencing and thinking during sessions of meditation. If one recognizes that confusion is one's main disturbance, then some good everyday advice would be: first thought, best thought. One should then simply do what is in front of one's nose and handle events one by one. Mind's ability to not be distracted thus evolves and will bring about inner clarity and strength.

Those who are drawn to the Great Perfection transform anger and pride best through the Father tantras. Here the building up phase where one lets the Buddha appear, is usually kept longer. This enables the meditator to comfortably check the details and make sure he remains in control. The completion phase, where one experiences deep openness, is kept short because it is often felt to be too close. In daily life, the best way to keep pride and anger at bay is to consciously develop compassion. Here the understanding that beings make their mistakes from stupidity rather than out of evil—and will also later suffer because of them—should be internalized.

"By knowing one, may we attain conviction in the realization of all."

Karmapa now returns to a matter of common concern, i.e., the fact that it is of secondary importance how the goal was reached. The most effective methods that people can use are the best ones.

Whichever one of Buddha's ways one chooses and whether desire, confusion, or anger produce the fuel, in the end all of Buddha's ultimate teachings lead first to liberation, and then to enlightenment. When the goal has been reached, all meditations and teachings are automatically realized. Karmapa sees the world like a man looking from the top of a mountain. He constantly experiences what is ultimate and at the same time shows varying beings the ways that lead them there.

Any combination of disturbing feelings may function as a gateway. With his 84,000 teachings in 108 heavy books, Buddha thought of everyone. Whether one prefers swimming in the ocean, examining a sample of water in a laboratory, or looking at its great expanse from an airplane, one learns to understand water.

THE ORAL TRANSMISSION Kagyu Lineage	THE VIRTUOUS ONES Gelugpa Lineage	THE OLD TRANSMISSION Nyingma Lineage
Main Tantra Mother tantra Short building up phase, long dissolving phase Wants to enjoy	**Main Tantra** Non-dual tantra Building up and completion phase of equal length Many details in order to keep mind focused	**Main Tantra** Father tantra Long building up and short completion phase in meditation Doesn't want to be betrayed
Insight Great Seal Realization very fast with the right blessing	**Insight** Great Middle Way Analysis The way is therefore slower and more drawn out	**Insight** Great Perfection View Development very quick if one can keep the highest view
Main Buddha Highest Bliss/Red Wisdom (Demchok Phagmo)	**Main Buddha** Secret Collection (Sangwa Dupa)	**Main Buddha** Diamond Dagger (Dorje Phurba)
Buddha Family Lotus Family	**Buddha Family** Buddha Family	**Buddha Family** Diamond Family
Main Disturbing Emotion Attachment	**Main Disturbing Emotion** Confusion	**Main Disturbing Emotion** Anger/Pride
Work on a daily basis Remembering impermanence. Spontaneously sharing good feelings with others	**Work on a daily basis** Less pondering, first thought best thought Following guidelines	**Work on a daily basis** To be aware of old age, sickness, death, and loss Thus developing compassion for beings

SAKYAPAS—not mentioned in the verse—are between Kagyupas and Gelugpas: Main Tantra—Mother tantra; Main Budhha—Oh Diamond (Kye Dorje/Hevajra)

ཞེན་པ་མེད་པའི་བདེ་ཆེན་རྒྱུན་ཆད་མེད།

Unceasing great bliss, free of attachment.

མཚན་འཛིན་མེད་པའི་འོད་གསལ་སྒྲིབ་གཡོགས་བྲལ།

Unobscured clarity, free of clinging to characteristics.

བློ་ལས་འདས་པའི་མི་རྟོགས་ལྷུན་གྱིས་གྲུབ།

Spontaneous non-conceptuality, beyond the intellect.

རྩོལ་མེད་ཉམས་སྐྱོང་རྒྱུན་ཆད་མེད་པར་ཤོག།

May these effortless experiences be continuous.

VERSE 20

Since enlightenment transcends concepts there are countless entry points to this verse. One should sometimes enjoy it from the angle of feeling and at other times mainly through comprehension. Here it again seems relevant to examine Karmapa's insights one by one. This is what words allow one to do best, and then every statement is liberating!

"Unceasing great bliss, free of attachment."

Karmapa's first wish points to the realization of mind's clarity, to the richness of its possibilities and its unobstructed free play. With these words he does not describe merely pleasant but impermanent states that are brought about through special conditions and are experienced as the opposite of frustration and suffering. Instead, he shows the limitless awareness of timeless mind, the deep ocean underneath the waves. As soon as true fearlessness has appeared, because one recognized one's own essence to be indestructible space, highest bliss simultaneously arises through mind's inherent clarity and power. It is the self-arisen surplus of space and experiences itself inwardly as a state of originality and freshness in every situation and as a blissful movement in the channels and wheels of one's energy system. Outwardly that same richness manifests as the pure lands of the buddhas, as well as the powerfields that constantly surround them. The buddhas and their energy fields appear at that moment when one directs one's first confident thought towards them or to the lama who represents them. When pronouncing the syllables of their mantras or invocations, they are there, whether one perceives them or not. On the vehicle of cause and effect, or the Theravada, the degree to which the Buddhas can help beings—and how quickly their blessing becomes active—depends on the amount of karmic hindrances the practitioners were able to remove. The compassionate practical methods and complete wisdom of emptiness of the Great Way vastly increase the ability of the Buddhas to influence beings' lives; and on the Diamond Way level they can often act directly. The practitioner's idealistic identification with enlightenment and the growth of the rainbow palaces of the Buddhas invoked around the meditators make the most direct of bonds. Eventually all separation between truth inside and out will have disappeared and the protectors and "Givers of Activity" (Skt. *Dakas* and *Dakinis,* Tib. *Pawo* and *Khandro)* are simply everywhere.

This state is recognized as expressing the radiant qualities of the experiencer and is comparable to a mirror, which is much more luminous and real than its changing images. It is the timeless ability to experience things essentially and directly— that particular mental freshness—which makes everything possible. Our finest qualities, be they love, joy, wisdom, courage, or power, were not given to mind from somewhere else. They are the timeless expression of its essence. Constantly playful and new, its space-clarity brings forth limitless possibilities. They unite form, sound, consciousness, and emptiness and make the world into a pure land.

Because its only cause is awareness, ultimate joy appears unceasingly and without effort. For this reason, it is also indestructible. Mind is forever radiant, and the discovery that there exists neither a real me nor an outer world means that one will not end up paralyzed in a black hole. Now, instead, there are no limits or hindrances to mind's freedom. On the absolute level it is not possible to negate or leave such purity. Whatever may happen to one's brain and nerves as transformers and carriers of consciousness, mind is no thing and cannot be harmed.

It has not been put together, but it is unlike a white wall that is blank when no pictures are projected upon it. Instead mind shines timelessly through its own power, like the sun. Through its own qualities, it experiences everything and effortlessly manifests the inner and outer worlds. Although the buddha fields of the joy-state can be felt more strongly at places where they were created and people later meditated, this changes nothing concerning the ultimate state of truth. It is always and everywhere. Whoever participates in a guided meditation (Tib. *gum lung*), meditates after receiving an initiation (Tib. *wang*), including the necessary permission (Tib. *lung*) and instructions (Tib. *tri*), or has received the transmission of the Great Seal, will create pure lands wherever he is. Mind is all-pervading. In its ultimate essence it is limitless potential that cannot be more in one place and less somewhere else. Therefore beings are already enlightened—they just have to find this out. Because truth nature pervades everything, everyone has always been a buddha. Even the very special methods used in the Diamond Way, can only remove the veils, which block mind's experience of itself. They can add nothing to truth itself. The moments when the experiencer first knows itself through the flow of its experiences strikes untrained mind by surprise, and one's bodily reaction may be very strong. They are like powerful rays of the sun that suddenly break through the clouds of one's habits and expectations. Whoever lives in accordance with common (Buddhist) sense, accumulates the necessary positive impressions, and empties his store-consciousness of harmful luggage, will increasingly feel drawn towards mind's absolute states. From the moment when one's concepts of an existent I or self have fallen away, that is liberation; and suffering has become something abstract. One is then no longer the target, and future development is secured. On the stretch up to the final union of subject, object, and action—enlightenment—the accomplisher will ever more discover his radiant essence. From then on, there exists only boundless significance, inside or outside.

However joyful these states may be, the increasing bliss of spiritual growth should not make one reject the conditioned joys of life. They create one's connections with others and are the frame for one's ability to benefit them. In comparison to the state of realization, however, such joys remain small. In the tip of his little finger a buddha continually experiences the joy lovers know from their best moments of union. Even the most wonderful conditioned states are only a shadow of the experience of timeless mind. The fulfillment that keeps unfolding from the level of liberation up to full enlightenment will spread ever more from one's meditation to one's whole life. At the end of one's way stands massive, unending bliss and a limitless "yes!" in response to existence.

"Unceasing great bliss, free of attachment."

Why is this so? Because the joy of realization surpasses all. Whoever stands in the full radiance of the sun will not notice the moon or the stars. Experienced from the immediate bliss of space, conditioned states of happiness are at most small additional gifts. As already mentioned, these joys are meaningful because they are shared; but one chooses to either get involved in them or not. As soon as mind's immeasurable and constant richness is recognized, conditioned experiences lose their ability to produce attachment. When highest joy is recognized to be the essence of all things, the attraction of conditioned phenomena disappears. Whoever rests in mind's essence will watch the world with amazement, seeing how beings make themselves dependent upon impermanent values and measuring the success of their lives by the amount of things they gather, keep, or throw away.

"Unobscured clarity free of clinging to characteristics."

That mind's clear light is also logical is a prospect that is only fondly dreamed about until the blessing of a teacher of the Great Seal kicks in. After a successful exchange, with increasing fearlessness, the students will see outer and inner events as a mirror and playground for their minds; and enlightenment will be only a question of dedication and time. Here it is useful to know that the experienced luminosity is not a light from somewhere else, but the perpetual flow of one's own "a-ha" experiences. Although inseparable from the experiencer, like waves from the ocean, still awareness and the dream-like and transient nature of these experiences is recognized to be mutually dependent: "empty of any own nature," as Buddha said. While the experiencer and its objects are brought to mirror and enrich one another through this insight, the wisdom of the Great Seal delivers the ultimate and enlightening quality: In essence they were always one, and they are expressions of that same all-knowing space. There exists no other realization than abiding in the limitless potential that encompasses all.

And just why is it that mind's clarity can have its timeless veils removed? Because the liberating power of the Great Seal is so convincing. After accepting this view and having known instances of mind's awesome power, one will still notice fragments of former concepts and habits floating by. Conditioned feelings and thoughts as well as any other dualistic experience should not be taken too seriously, however. They can only darken one's mind if one allows oneself to be limited by them. Leaving them to do their own thing while one does what one wants is like letting a thief come to an empty house. He will soon want to go elsewhere.

As no new insights can be added to absolute truth, each level of Buddha's teachings has only one goal: to remove hindrances to enlightenment and to convince mind of its true essence. When no disturbing feelings veil mind's clarity, one is liberated and everything becomes a pure land! Practicing from this secure level, fixed concepts can do nothing but disappear, skillful actions become spontaneous, and with the push of deep compassion one reaches the all-pervading radiance of enlightenment. Here the experiencer recognizes itself as unlimited intuitive space and every experience is rich and pure. Thoughts are clicked in and out as desired, being no longer difficult masters but now useful servants. They are kept ready for possible deployment, but one never allows them to limit the freshness of the here and now.

"Free of clinging to characteristics."

Why does highest bliss not need defining? Because its origin, space, needs nothing from anywhere. Being the wisdom that unites all things as well as the basis for anything outer or inner, there is nothing to prove and nobody else to prove it to. Whoever recognizes the radiance of the mirror behind its images or fathoms the depths of the ocean below its waves does not therefore lose the images or waves of the conditioned world. From his newly found and timeless state of richness, he can enjoy the various pictures and surf the waves more freely. The recognition of their interesting characteristics is, however, always easy and without attachment—because something else might also be quite appealing. Any moment is in itself a great gift, and no clinging has any meaning. One is already much richer than anything one could dream of. Whoever experiences mind to be unveiled and in essence indestructible, clear light needs nothing more and is automatically free. Depending on what is reasonable and beneficial for others, he may appreciate events to be pleasant or difficult; but there is no compulsion to do so. On the absolute level, everything is essentially pure anyway and of value simply because it happens. One acts from the feeling of oneness and for the good of others.

"Non-conceptuality beyond the intellect."

Without any separation between experiencer, object, and action, every situation is spontaneous. On the relative level, one then acts joyfully and without hesitation, from a full awareness of the "here-and-now," while on the highest levels the rich and undisturbed views of "both-and" watch over and give direction to events. Through this realization, the truth-nature of space and all things that appear in it is seen; and everything now appears from a state of surplus. Mind's radiant light needs no endorsement and is beyond any imagination. Thus, unmasked and beyond expectations and fear, the non-conceptual state appears by itself. Everything is now experienced in its timeless freshness.

"Spontaneous." Many Zen books were based on this word, and we can all recall examples of successful effortlessness. After a week of trying to hit the wastebasket, one's wish recedes. Then, without thinking, one scrunches a page up, does not bother to aim, and has success. Or as mentioned before, one often knows who is calling before hearing their voice or receives a letter from somebody one has just thought of. Such events stretch the laws of probability and show space to be a container that unites everything and communicates between beings. It also teaches one to trust what is. In moments without expectation one is actually more in the situation than when deeply pondering a subject. The Great Seal and the meditations of the Diamond Way most effectively produce experiences of oneness that open up one's potential and remain for ever-longer periods of time. When one applies the approach of "either-or" to daily life, one sees it as simply showing more focused possibilities of mind. The experience of essential freedom remains like the wide-open shiny space around everything after a parachute jump. As mind was both present and confused since beginningless time—not realizing subject, object, and action to be interdependent—it needs a great deal of practice in order to recognize itself in the way described above. Therefore, Karmapa's last piece of advice is to train and direct it by making many wishes. Remembering that there is no enlightenment for the lazy one gets the hard but necessary work done and arrives in a state of highest bliss where one can work steadily and without effort for the benefit of others—who could want for more?

9th Karmapa, Wangchuk Dorje, 1556–1603

བཟང་ཞེན་ཉམས་ཀྱི་འཛིན་པ་རང་སར་གྲོལ།

The clinging to the "good" experiences, to which we have become attached, dissolves on its own.

ངན་རྟོག་འཁྲུལ་པ་རང་བཞིན་དབྱིངས་སུ་དག

The illusion of "bad" thoughts is purified in the expanse of mind.

ཐ་མལ་ཤེས་པ་སྤང་བླང་བྲལ་ཐོབ་མེད།

Simple consciousness is free of giving up or adopting, of avoiding or obtaining.

སྤྲོས་བྲལ་ཆོས་ཉིད་བདེན་པ་རྟོགས་པར་ཤོག།

May we realize the truth-nature of phenomena free from all limiting constructs.

Verse 21

"The clinging to the 'good' experiences, to which we have become attached, dissolves on its own."

Once again the importance of a previous verse makes Karmapa bring us back to several of its statements. Enlightenment is timeless, highest bliss; but it still has room for the ordinary and conditioned joys of life. It is an easy state. Although Buddhism encourages people to share and be generous, it knows no guilt about feeling good or being successful. It even stresses that, if one continuously avoids the fruits of one's good karma, such as an enjoyable life-style, it will diminish. On the other hand, once one has tasted the joy of mind, worldly pleasures hold one much less tightly than before. Later on, as one moves closer to knowing mind, the memory of its radiance outshines other things; and after reaching the higher levels of the Great Seal, the value of experiences depends on their ability to mirror one's potential, placing meditation and extreme sports very high on the list. Finally, there is no alternative to lasting values and the bliss of full enlightenment. One is happy with whatever happens.

Here, one moves through the states of awareness that are aptly described by the terms "one pointedness," "non-artificiality," "one taste of all phenomena," and on to enlightened "non-meditation," which appear from mind itself. The levels of joy and meaning experienced here are so pervasive that one must first think of the needs of others—after all one is doing so well oneself. Here the words of many accomplishers bear one another out. Because ultimately everything is perfect anyway, one only needs to let go to have true fulfillment!

How can it be that **the illusion of 'bad' thoughts is purified in the expanse of mind"?** Because they are not separate from mind, which is clear light. They appear and develop in its space, are known through its clarity-awareness, and disappear again in its unlimited essence. The main point here may be difficult to understand when one has to deal with people on a practical daily level. One has to remind oneself that, although the capacity for abstract thinking of nations and individuals differs widely, this is only one aspect of mind's potential. If one adds feelings, memory, dreams, imagination, and artistic expression to its possibilities, mind has no limitation. Nothing can exist separate from mind.

To obtain such a liberating view, which brings true composure, it is vital to not judge oneself because of bad thoughts. They are conditioned anyway. If Schwarzenegger's films would be shown in the world's knitting-circles, then there would be an increase in the number of needle-stick injuries among these noble ladies. Instead one should be aware of thoughts and enjoy them when possible but without any clinging. One may know their playful richness or just let them dissolve. They are mind, and mind is clear light. Thus, even the strongest feelings and the most disturbing experiences are essentially pure.

On the absolute level of pure view, thoughts and feelings are seen to express mind's inherent wisdom. One should consider the unpleasant ones like waves that a surfer would simply not ride or a show on TV so bad that no one would watch it. The Tibetan expression is: "Like a dead cow"—one only glances once. Disturbing feelings have neither arms nor legs, are untraceable except as a disturbance in one's inner chemistry and only have the power we invest in them. One is certainly not facing a twelve-foot tall, eight hundred pound gorilla. The fact that one does not need to suffer because of one's feelings helps many people. A wise man never gives so much reality to his trips that they can unbalance him from his center and force him to do or say things against his will. From one's first meditation, and in spite of the necessary purification that will occur, conditions will allow one to create an ever safer distance from one's feelings. This is the main point in Karmapa's first two lines. Only those who become conscious that whatever arose must again dissolve, while at the same time knowing that mind is in its essence perfect, can skillfully avoid the unpleasant roles in life and instead repeatedly get to play the good ones. Approaching the highest level of insight, one will also have a healthy laugh at the show.

If confidence is based on the basic goodness behind mind's unlimited expression, one's handling of situations changes. Even with modern tragedies—like overpopulation in poor countries, the ghettos in our own towns, and the almost criminal naivety of governments full of do-gooders, still causing such massive and degrading suffering—one will look to solve the causes before spreading the blame. One works best beyond the simple concepts of "evil" and "sin" that come from contract religions. Instead, one thinks of what is or is not useful for beings and of whether it is at all possible to humanize a particular culture. Fearlessly, one observes every kind of activity and then decides with the long-term benefit of many in mind, even when an initially unpleasant cure appears necessary. Holding this view becomes easier with the certitude that mind was always essentially perfect. One's knowledge that everything lacking or painful is a faulty program, or less than genuine, allows disturbing influences to exhaust themselves, because of one's lack of involvement.

Three life-pervading levels of Buddhist practice unite thought, words, and action to benefit both others and oneself. First, if a beginner feels weak in a given situation, he should be aware of cause and effect and avoid scenarios, such as friends with drugs, where he would surely make mistakes. Although this may not look particularly heroic, if he openly admits to himself and others that this is necessary, then everybody learns.

Second, whoever worked with mind in this or former lives, or did many good things, has more depth and staying-power now and should further strengthen his motivation to benefit others. On this level, it is important to be conscious of the dream-like and changing nature of all problems. Informed by an intelligent and not politically-correct daily newspaper, one can become a useful friend for the countless uneducated people worldwide who are not free and are visibly doing much worse than oneself.

In the ultimate view of the Great Seal and the Great Perfection, the third and highest level of handling disturbing mental states is traditionally illustrated with stories and picturesque language. One lets "the thief come to an empty house" and "gives one's enemies neither nourishment nor respect." Continuously focused on what one is doing, one treats one's trouble like the elephant pricked by thorns. The thorns are there, but elephants have very thick skin. After multiple performances in a variety of costumes and with little success, the disturbing feelings simply stay away. They lose their power and virulence, and one may even assign them to certain tasks. When anger fades, one can use its residual energy consciously to complete daily chores like washing the dishes. With jealousy one may clean the toilet; and when confusion dissolves, one can answer one's mail. Whatever strange trips may still be lurking subconsciously, with this kind of treatment they will eventually leave. The ultimate view that only mind is real, being space and awareness inseparable, brings timeless enlightenment.

This approach is fundamentally different from the ideas of faith-religions, which only perceive mind's passing manifestations. Even their bravest attempts to retain "good" thoughts and avoid the "bad" ones will fail, and the effort required stresses mind. Most wisely, Buddha chose to focus on mind's timeless aspect as the basis for his work. The mirror, the ocean, and the experiencer are his goal, not the constantly changing images, waves, and experiences. What is useful and harmful, including gods and devils, are just passing appearances in the timeless space of mind. Instead, one is fascinated by the boundless blissful essence from which every event arises, which is aware of everything, and into which all things return. Naturally, during this search for mind's essence one moves skillfully in the world; and every action is guided by the wish to benefit others. Such an exciting process should meet as few outer obstacles as possible. Among all available methods, the Diamond Way meditations—like the Foundational Practices, the Way of Identification with one's teacher or buddha form, and the view of the Great Seal—are the most effective at removing unpleasant seeds from mind. Regular short and inspiring sessions rather than long, dreary, or infrequent ones, especially of the "Guru Yogas," are one's lifeline to enlightened nature in any situation.

Also, Karmapa's statement about beings' "simple consciousness" could only have been given by a Buddhist and can only be understood by kindred spirits. In other traditions the subject is processed. One looks for the "pure" mind, the "Atman-Brahman," the "cleaned self," the "righteous soul," the "spiritual I" or whatever else is currently in vogue, not to mention the countless expressions of the different schools of psychology. It was precisely this letting go of anything artificial, the discarding of ideas that could not be tested, and the avoidance of pretentious explanations that say nothing—that enabled Buddha to get enlightened. Still today, mind needs nothing other than itself for this greatest of tasks. Therefore Karmapa singularly focuses on the experiencer, that it must recognize itself. Its unlimited aware space accommodates all phenomena and skills, and it neither has to abandon anything to avoid being defective nor to add something to improve itself. Mind's essence was always indestructible accomplishment, contained everything and need not therefore obtain anything. The reason for all of Buddha's eighty-four thousand teachings and the many kinds of meditation is only one: to let mind experience its oneness and unlimited nature.

That is the goal. Standing like a broad oak tree, one's power is unshakable. At the same time, one humorously observes the circus of the conditioned world pass by and compassionately intervenes whenever it is meaningful and karmically possible. Whoever manages to achieve this will even benefit beings unintentionally and has attained everything.

15th Karmapa, Khakyab Dorje, 1871–1922

འགྲོ་བའི་རང་བཞིན་རྟག་ཏུ་སངས་རྒྱས་ཀྱང་།

The nature of beings is always Buddha.

མ་རྟོགས་དབང་གིས་མཐའ་མེད་འཁོར་བར་འཁྱམས།

Yet, not realizing this, they wander in the endless cycle of
conditioned existence.

སྡུག་བསྔལ་མུ་མཐའ་མེད་པའི་སེམས་ཅན་ལ།

May the limitless pain of all beings awaken an overwhelming
compassion in our minds.

བཟོད་མེད་སྙིང་རྗེ་རྒྱུད་ལ་སྐྱེ་བར་ཤོག

The nature of beings is always the state of Buddha.

VERSE 22

After spanning mind's potential with these central verses, which convey the radiance of Buddha's absolute wisdom, Karmapa now prepares to land. To do this under the most noble of circumstances, he first gives a brief reminder of the enlightenment inherent in all beings. Without losing its freshness, he wants to bring the view of the Great Seal into the world of activity.

But how? He might have used the runways of powerful action or discriminating wisdom; but, in accordance with the stream of his reincarnations, he touches down on compassion. His enlightening view may best enter the world through the broad bridges of this most precious of motivations.

With his practical experience, Karmapa does not over-estimate his chances of making a realization of the above profundity widely understood. Both in countries like Tibet (where it was available for nine hundred years) and also now in the West, such an all-encompassing view is too much for most people to grasp. On the other hand, it is a conviction shared among the practitioners of the Great Seal that beings are in actual fact very close to that state! Initially this under-standing manifests as moments of wonder, joy, and amaze-ment; but gradually and from a certain stage of development on, a growing conviction solidifies. One feels that it is only necessary for beings to momentarily open their eyes to expe-rience the same richness that one lives oneself: that every atom actually vibrates with joy and is kept together by love.

That the limitless clarity of space inherent in everybody, their awareness, is that of a perfect Buddha.

Whoever can see the world from the level of highest purity and deepest meaning is amazed at what beings make of their buddha nature. It is then disturbing to see how much unnecessary pain they bring to others and themselves and how much of their joyful potential they miss out on. However, Karmapa stays with mind's possibilities and produces art for art's sake. He mentions none of the actual suffering of seven hundred years ago and does not call for any action. Although he certainly helps people to understand that one's use of the laws of cause and effect is the key to a better life and that it is about opportunity, not fate, he does not tell them how to handle difficulties. This possibly implies that he is addressing a cultural environment in which there are already rules concerning what is considered acceptable behavior. It may also have been due to the living conditions at his time, where people felt far weaker than now. They were therefore quick to submit to the restricting circumstances of a world that was more threatening and not nearly as transparent as the one enjoyed today. Buddha saw his monks as examples to bring to people's attention the causes of their situation, but he did not wish them to actually interfere with other people's lives. Side-stepping the practical details concerning society and people's behavior, Karmapa instead returns to the ultimate cause of all pain, the dualistic view of unenlightened beings. He points to the separation experienced between experiencer, object experienced, and act of experiencing.

Except for the very first verses and that of verse 16, where the topic was mental calmness, Karmapa taught solely on the level of the Diamond Way. The endless cycle of birth and death, as well as all other events, appear as mind's free, joyful, and self-liberating play. He wrote for the brave people who live for the benefit of others and meditate on the right teachings. He also celebrated the lucky ones fascinated by the view of the Great Seal. With this verse he now gears down into the conditions experienced by ordinary beings, which are so precisely depicted on the Tibetan "Wheel of Life." His presentation of tightness and egotism fits closely with the experience of those who feel caught up in a life with few dimensions. The further one gets from enlightenment, the narrower conditioned situations become. Karmapa's compassion embraces all those who do not recognize their own nature and therefore have no part in mind's greatness and bliss. Ignorance is as timeless as mind itself; and Buddha sees its cause, not as a personal expulsion from a paradise, but as mind's inability to recognize itself. When enlightenment is reached, times and directions are infinite; but the ways that lead to this state are well trodden and clearly defined.

But what is this beginningless, but not endless, "Wheel of Life"? And why is it so difficult to escape? The reason is always the same: Mind is like an eye that cannot see itself but instead notices everything that appears. Its space-essence therefore understands itself to be an "I" and because of this, its clarity-awareness, that which is experienced, becomes a "you" or something else. From the experience of this illusory duality appears attachment, ill will, and all the mixed feelings that are able to fool mind because of its lack of distance and absolute view. These feelings lead to untimely words and actions that again bring about awkward and damaging results. Although everybody produces their own situation, one still places the causes of suffering with others. One then acts or speaks against them and starts a further round of difficult exchange.

This wheel turns without end until a buddha appears and shows beings how they function. The methods he gives enable them to find freedom and then enlightenment. Here, one stops looking for happiness elsewhere as it is all within oneself. Being mind's spontaneous and effortless space, it never left.

The **"suffering"** that was mentioned has to be seen in the light of the religions of experience from the Far East. As something totally harmful must self-destruct due to the laws of causality, its origin is understood to be stupidity rather than evil as the dramatic religions of revelation, contract, and faith from the Middle East would have one believe. It can therefore be removed through one's own power, although a bit of help is nice. These are important points to know, because Buddha's first Noble Truth, "there exists suffering" has upset many of his most inspired students over the last two thousand five hundred and fifty years. In fact, it was given to five joyless ascetics of the kind who would also today shun the Diamond Way. This is why it is not easy for people who feel satisfied in life to sense the purpose of this teaching. If one thinks for a while, however, his words reveal themselves to be most promising. After all, everything is relative and the evaluation of an experience is a question of what one is used to or compares it with. Alongside the timeless highest bliss of enlightenment that is inherent in all beings and which Buddha sees, even the most pleasant conditioned joys or the most fulfilling moments are less satisfying and are therefore a form of suffering. His standard is what accomplishers of all times have described as the unceasing state of immeasurable bliss, which appears spontaneously and gives direct meaning to every experience. After a few years on the Diamond Way one cannot imagine living without the wonderful taste of this potential.

Recognizing mind's clear light is unimaginable happiness. As this perfection is the timeless, indestructible essence of all beings, Buddhists who are concerned with world affairs speak openly and with a clear conscience when it comes to thorny issues. Politically incorrect jokes or critical statements are made not from dislike but only to awaken people and save everybody from future embarrassment and pain. After all, it is only those with a bad conscience that feel attacked, and as long as one's assertions are factually based, everybody should be thankful. The expression of an honest opinion does not make anybody small or poor. On the contrary, beings are thus made to notice the hindrances that keep them from improving their outer and inner lives.

The expression **"the limitless pain of all beings"** strikes self-assured holders of modern Western "can-do" cultures as being rather emotional. It is also not in keeping with Karmapa's usual style, as one finds no complaints elsewhere in the text. Nevertheless, the vast majority of the world's population lives in poverty. Even in the rich countries with low birth rates and high standards of education there is still a massive amount of suffering in various institutions. According to Buddha's teachings, however, humans are generally well off. The realms of animals, of ghosts, and the states of paranoia that are called hell are far more unpleasant.

Compassion is appropriate but should not be confused with pity, which keeps people small and robs them of the chance to lift themselves out of their situation. Here it is meaningful for everyone to consciously build up positive impressions and remove the roots of future suffering through working for the benefit of others. The unifying factor here should be the realization that everybody has buddha nature. It also pays to understand that during one's countless lives one has surely experienced every kind of situation oneself and that difficulties will surely appear if one stays unconscious and continues to harm beings.

Although there exist ways to reach liberation without compassion, they are slow and one absolutely needs the hands of all beings pushing one forward to accomplish enlightenment. In addition to this, one cannot avoid expressing one's feelings of oneness with beings, which continuously increase, bringing about generous and heart-warming acts. While one's view remains the inborn purity of the Diamond Way, few can share that; and one's activity will have to be on the level of the Great Way, which balances compassion and wisdom. Understanding that one can do little for others if confused or in pain oneself, it involves the decision to reach enlightenment for the good of all. Together with the overflowing toolbox of the Diamond Way methods and view, there is no limit to what a hard working man can do.

Tibetans sometimes give three practical examples of how to benefit others. A king, a ferryman, and a shepherd may all do something good but probably their motivation will differ. The king possibly thinks: "When I have reached a strong position, I will help the others." The ferryman wishes that all may reach the shore safely together, and the shepherd first wants to get his flock home. The world needs all three kinds of motivation. Everybody should begin with what they can do now and then later spread themselves further afield, otherwise things become artificial. Although the king, can benefit most through his actions and the ferryman will enjoy the richness of shared human goals, the shepherd often has the best results. Whoever thinks of himself has problems, but whoever thinks of others has interesting jobs to do. The greatest trick of all is simply to forget oneself.

 རིགས་ཀུན་ཁྱབ་བདག་རྡོ་རྗེ་འཆང་།

Dorje Chang

བཅོད་མེད་སྙིང་རྗེའི་རྩལ་ཡང་མ་འགགས་པའི།

When overwhelming compassion expresses itself without being obstructed,

བརྩེ་དུས་ངོ་བོ་སྟོང་དོན་རྗེན་པར་འར།

its empty nature shines forth in the moment of love.

ཟུང་འཇུག་གོལ་ས་བྲལ་བའི་ལམ་མཆོག་འདི།

May we never deviate from this supreme and faultless way of unity,

འབྲལ་མེད་ཉིན་མཚན་ཀུན་ཏུ་བསྒོམ་པར་ཤོག།

but practice it day and night.

VERSE 23

The wheels have now touched the tarmac and Karmapa is deciding which gate to approach. The goal is now to integrate enlightened insight into daily life, and compassion evidently was a wise point of entry. The healthy, generous kind of love is represented in Tibetan Buddhism by the giving position of the lower right hand of Liberatrice (Skt. *Tara*, Tib. *Dolma*)—which gives the refuge of Buddha, his teachings, and one's stable companions on the way—and by the four arms of the Bodhisattva Loving Eyes. This trusting feeling, beyond any stickiness or anticipation, naturally falls into four spheres: love, when one gives and receives effortlessly; compassion, when one gives more (but that is fine because the receiver is developing); sympathetic joy, when something meaningful happens elsewhere and one shares in it joyfully; and finally equanimity, the certainty that all beings have the buddha nature—no matter how bizarrely they behave. This understanding makes one's work with others meaningful: one is cleaning a diamond and not a piece of coal.

Working with such complicated states of mind, how does Karmapa find a way around emotionality or nannying his students? Here, and more importantly than elsewhere, it depends on the type of action he uses. In the countries where Buddha's teachings were known for centuries, the mild smile of a holy man may have been effective in drawing people away from meaningless habits, while somebody who enters a life-long retreat may inspire reverent whispers and bring donations for the monastery. In Western cultures, however, where Buddhism now lives and grows in people's lives, something practical and transparent is expected. The above types of expression are not easily understood and may even freak some people out. In the street, in bed, or at the office, compassion should be seen as useful, conscious actions that are best generated when holding the view of the Great Seal and meditating each day. If one wishes to touch modern Westerners on a large scale, then one's approach must not embarrass them by working with fear or being sticky and sweet. Otherwise those independent and intelligently critical people who could only be satisfied with the Diamond Way level of teaching will have nowhere else to go, and basically good teachers will receive only fleeting visits by the curious or unstable. They will then find themselves forced to pass on their best teachings to students who would be better off with gods who tell them what to do.

Buddha's wisdom should of course always be available through all media, given in accordance with beings' understanding and fitting the given situation. Making the wish to develop in an ever-increasing but also secure way, and for every action to be guided by wisdom—this is forward thinking and mature. Therefore, it is meaningful to activate one's outer, inner, and secret teachers. Together they touch all aspects of a person and bring about total development (see verse 5).

The "outer" teacher is the person who makes one trust one's buddha nature, on whichever level that may happen. He gives the liberating and enlightening teachings and meditations and inspires one by his trustworthy example. Though his energy field pervades all the centers he starts, one still needs to meet with him from time to time to be sure that one is on track. He can quickly guide one away from becoming proud, sentimental, or cold-bloodedly intellectual. The teacher is the best mirror for one's mind. If one simply feels relaxed and at home in his presence or at the centers that express his activity, this is a sign of a healthy development. One should avoid having anything to hide from the teacher or from oneself.

The "inner" teacher consists of the instructions received and the maturity one obtains by using them. They must be authentically Buddhist and absolutely exclude elements of New Age, Hinduism, esoteric Christianity—or even worse: any mixture of all these that pleases one's ego. Instead, the inner teacher should be like the chorus in the ancient Greek tragedies, showing mind what is actually going on. This flow of insight that closely follows events makes them useful. It explains them on the level of karma as well as within the framework of one's general development.

The secret teacher is something total and may surprise one powerfully like an electric shock. It is that luminous insight that appears inseparably from the experience, the great "a-ha," which unites and understands everything in a moment of radiant wisdom. Mind's clear light is nothing outer. It is the unbroken stream of these self-arising realizations. No greater fulfillment exists! When such insights are constant and beyond-personal, that is enlightenment.

How can one express these three teachers at once? The trick is to not make compassion into a "something" but simply to act from the feeling of the moment. Whoever experiences the smallest possible separation between subject, object, and action—while skillfully using the methods of Buddha that fit the situation—will be right, while anything stilted will not work. Outwardly, one should trust one's life-experience. This means causing the minimum of suffering to the fewest possible beings while speaking and acting for the greatest long-term benefit of all. Inwardly, the goal is a healthy sense of humor to keep things fresh. This allows one to skillfully balance compassion and wisdom for the good of all. The secret level is perfected by abiding in the experience of space and bliss as inseparable. One experiences the buddha essence of all beings, the fundamental truth and the nowness of all events, and acts spontaneously and effectively.

Kunzig Sharmapa, the right hand of the Karmapa incarnations from their beginning, compares the view of the Great Seal to drawing a picture in water. Everything fits in the moment, as it is, but in the process of appearing it also immediately frees itself. This is also the nature of enlightened action. It is here and now, beyond expectations or fear, without clinging or avoiding.

The oneness of compassion and emptiness is called the faultless way. In addition to the reasons mentioned elsewhere, it is also because all beings and situations are interdependent that nothing completely egocentric can exist. By benefiting oneself in reasonable ways, one will automatically also benefit others. Through this realization, duality becomes only relative; and good actions take on a beyond-personal nature. This suffocates any disturbing pride beneath mountains of joyful tasks. Soon, one will be far too busy for any such feelings, and making future achievements happen will be much more wonderful than any previously obtained!

Nowhere does one encounter any real limits. Whoever would like to effortlessly extend this trust in space that graces their day also into the night, can continue their experience of mind with a "Clear Light" meditation that is taught in the Diamond Way Buddhist centers. If one uses it in a very natural and relaxed way, parts of one's sleep can become a further joyful experience of mind's potential. Here one may recognize mind's self-empowering, conscious space. As this verse puts some emphasis on practice during the night, which is unusual, here is a little further information. The Diamond Way meditation mentioned above expands awareness on many levels. If during a dream one manages to hold, and later extend into all moments of one's life, the understanding that one is dreaming, one will actually become enlightened. Mind is then fully conscious and recognizes itself unfettered by time and space. Dreams of Buddhas, one's teachers, and whatever else points to mind's timeless essence are good signs that mind's veils are thinning and that one is approaching their state. Awareness during the night also pays off on the relative level. One's ability to continue the dreamy, unreal feeling of the night into the day gives first-class protection against suffering. From then on, one will notice with growing relief that the difficulties bugging one were not present before, that they change constantly now, and that they will also surely pass. One's daily practice of view and meditation brings effects at night and gradually enables one to direct one's dreams. As sleep studies at the University of Chicago in May 2002 show, those who have meditated for many years sleep deeper than others but subjectively feel more conscious. It is an important point because, as this quality of awareness develops, one also becomes able to hold on to the clear light during the process of dying. This enables one to reach enlightenment when all the energies meet in one's heart-center between twenty and thirty minutes after one's last breath.

སྒོམ་སྟོབས་ལས་བྱུང་སྤྱན་དང་མངོན་ཤེས་དང་།

Through the powers and insights arising from meditation,

སེམས་ཅན་སྨིན་བྱེས་སངས་རྒྱས་ཞིང་རབ་སྦྱངས།

may we mature beings, train in the buddhas´ pure lands
and perfect the aspiration to attain the buddha qualities.

སངས་རྒྱས་ཆོས་རྣམས་འགྲུབ་པའི་སྨོན་ལམ་རྫོགས།

After accomplishing the steps of maturing others, training, and

རྫོགས་སྨིན་སྦྱངས་གསུམ་མཐར་ཕྱིན་སངས་རྒྱས་ཤོག།

perfection, may we reach buddhahood.

VERSE 24

As Karmapa approaches the end of these verses, he points out the different qualities that will naturally arise after a good deal of practice. In well-educated Buddhist circles, it is unusual to speak about extrasensory powers; they are regarded like money in high society. One has it and doesn't speak about it but has the valet park one's expensive car. At the same time, however, his words prove how hands-on he can be and how close the Great Seal is to real life. The most important thing to him is the welfare of all beings. He is not interested in a morality that is imposed from the outside or used to control others. What he wants is his student's development, so he will share what he finds to be useful knowledge for them. Nine hundred years ago, Marpa and Milarepa were also not modest. They performed miracles like a magician pulling rabbits from his hat. Today, believers in materialism continue to be amazed how frequently weather patterns change at large Diamond Way events such as at the inaugurations of stupas and the initiations given by teachers like Lopon Tsechu Rinpoche as well as the Phowa courses, where since 1987 about fifty thousand Westerners have learned how to die consciously. Often at the beginning and end of these gatherings there are spontaneous rainbows, strong gusts of wind, or sudden downpours of rain. Seeing them tie-in very closely with events and limited to the immediate vicinity made several new and scientifically minded students think of asking for a refund on their school fees.

The realm of unusual occurrences may in fact be much closer than people usually assume when they are busily caught up in their stressful lives. Whoever recognizes this from a healthy state of mind is usually already very bright and experiences a great deal of happy excitement in life. Many people completely avoid this issue, however. They feel it to be too shadowy, superstitious, controlling their lives, and full of potentially embarrassing surprises.

As mind and the world evidently influence one another and seem to be in essence inseparable, one should obtain for oneself a relaxed relationship to this sort of phenomenon at an early stage. As they will anyway tug at one's mind-stream ever more frequently in the course of one's development, it is useful to understand just what an openness to mind's beyond-materialistic potential entails. This subject matter is seldom touched upon but is nonetheless exciting and worth further explanation.

First, one may distinguish between two kinds of miracles, depending on whether or not they are based on an understanding of mind's ultimate nature. The first kind are the liberating actions that belong to the great accomplishers and Buddhas who realized during former lives that their sensory awareness was conditioned. From this basis follows a growing recognition that the world of appearance is simply the condensed common karmic thought patterns of beings. Or to put it another way, one first succeeds in recognizing that one's own experiences are impermanent and change like dreams whether they happen during the day or at night (see verse 23). Then, one can take the next step and focus on the condensed karmic dream that is the present outer world of one's senses. As it consists of constantly shifting conditions, it is also not real and one is therefore not at its mercy. It can be worked with and changed.

Continuing with the enlightened side to miracles, one's power in this area appears from promises made during former lives, much meditation, and of course the karmic density of the beings one wishes to help. From a state of freedom one wisely chooses to work in the areas one knows best and where further karmic connections exist. Such beyond-personal actions that benefit the world express the Buddha's peace-giving, increasing, fascinating, and powerfully protective energy fields and appear whenever needed or even when one only thinks of them. They influence the outer world and make the pure lands appear. Probably the most frequently described miracles of this kind are the situations where someone's life was saved in a convincing and unexpected manner. My book *Riding the Tiger*,[1] which is about the development of living Buddhism in the West, contains several such cases where the outer influence of a force of great compassion came tangibly close. Spontaneous realizations of great meaning and unexpected capabilities also belong in this realm. They are a joyful, loving expression of mind's limitless richness and self-liberating qualities. Manifesting from the vibrations of different Buddhas and accomplishers, they protect and bless beings whenever and wherever possible. Whoever has had the joy of meeting a buddha as an energy form knows that no other happiness compares.

This area of self-arisen powerfields or of "outer" blessing can become active wherever people's habitual minds don't block the work of positive energies. Although blessing sounds quite church-like, there doesn't seem to exist a better word for this phenomenon. Space is not only wisdom, it is joy and love as well. Whenever possible, it enables one's potential to ripen. It is also not a black hole—or where something is

1. Lama Ole Nydahl, *Riding the Tiger.* (Nevada City, CA: Blue Dolphin, 1992).

missing—but instead it is a container. It supplies the enlightened view, the wisdoms and useful actions that are oriented towards the future. Everything and everybody is held by it, surrounded by it, and connected through it. It is therefore neither necessary to die in order to experience a pure land nor to go elsewhere to meet Buddhas; purifying one's mind and keeping maximum consciousness is enough. Nothing but this enlightened space expresses itself as inner and outer perfection, as the bliss felt by doing good actions, and as meaningful miracles in nature and our everyday world.

There are several reasons why so many Westerners today can progress successfully on the Diamond Way. In particular, the transmissions brought to our countries from the early seventies are a great treasure. They were passed on by several representatives of the lineages of accomplishment and were usually pure and unbroken. Though few are aware of this fact, Kunzig Sharmapa, an authority on Tibetan lineages and transmissions, tells us that Tibetan Buddhism didn't keep its power over the last nine hundred and fifty years inside the monasteries. They easily became infested with politics and were often the seats of administration. It was instead in the caves where accomplishers lived freely and tasted life and meditation to the full. There also existed checking and self-purifying mechanisms. Even when some lineage holders and other Rinpoches with yard-long collections of titles failed on a practical human level, believing where they should have questioned and recently being co-opted by those who simultaneously destroyed the last cultural vestiges of their country, little harm happened. People were able to separate the teachers from the treasures they passed on and, with the strength of the many initiations that had been given, stayed. When Westerners gave up on such teachers because of these failings or other more personal ones, they usually also did it for idealistic reasons and with little ill will. As this process was not detrimental to anyone, the powerfields that had been generated were also not lost.

What the Uri Gellers or Ted Serios of this world display—and probably also what Sai Baba shows his students—are miracles that belong to the second category. Such "worldly" events appear through a particularly strong ability to focus mind. This generates outer as well as inner events from the endless possibilities of space. The type of meditation that brings them about is the previously mentioned *shi-ne* or *shamatha*, which literally means calming and holding mind in one place (see verse 16). The benefit derived from wonders such as these depends on the maturity of those who produce them as well as those who witness them.

Whatever form of spontaneous or desired wonders appear, they are a good sign as long as one manages to avoid pride. Whether one brings forth their basis through a state of confidence and thankfulness through which the Buddha can work or searches for them through one-pointed concentration, the level of absorption that makes them possible is the finest ground for one's further meditation. It is of little meaning, however, to direct such massive energies towards worldly gains. Trying to force one's own development before the foundation is established is also harmful, and focusing one-pointedly to obtain states of absorption that are strong enough to bend karma for lesser goals inside the conditioned world leads to great stress on the body. Some have been known to bleed from their intestines while others can hardly see for hours after such a session. In addition, only those results that have ripened in one's mind-stream and fit with conditions are truly useful and lasting. Although such stories abound in Tibet, the value of producing this second kind of miracle as a means to convince others is limited; and the excitement remains effective only in the short term. For this purpose, the four thoughts at the beginning of any meditation is all one needs!

One's manipulation of the world of appearance only impresses those who are already open to wonders. Out of mental laziness, most prefer to stay convinced that one did in fact have something tucked up one's sleeve after all. In the final analysis, probably only those ready for a major jump in their development can have any real benefit. This is why signs of influencing causality are called "ordinary" miracles, while acts turning beings' minds from pain to meaning are the "extraordinary" ones. Real accomplishment is felt by all and manifests through one's motivations and control of mind.

Although one should certainly try any skillful method available to shake beings from their fixed ideas of living in a solid world, the most attractive example remains visible human growth. Nothing else is truly convincing. The demonstrations of miracles with no ultimate purpose does not develop one any further, and people's time is certainly too short to waste. Excessive striving for supernatural abilities or signs are an expression of immaturity and will eventually get in the way of one's development as a complete being. Instead of generating expectations and pressure, the Buddhas advise one to abide effortlessly in an authentic and properly understood meditation. In the Diamond Way these methods should be obtained through a guided meditation, *gum lung* from a lama or one of his groups, or through an initiation, *wang,* a permission *lung* and an instruction *tri* from a lama with a genuine transmission.

Newcomers should find the time to speak to the experienced people in the center they frequent and learn from the books and videos that are available. However, on the Diamond Way and concerning the teachings on "emptiness," one should take care not to mix instructions from different schools. All the traditions are beneficial and have great masters; but lineage-hopping leads to troublesome confusion, as much terminology and even the understanding of space differs between even the schools of Tibetan Buddhism. The three old "Red Hat" schools here hold the view experienced by meditators using the whole mind. In Tibetan, their word is *shentong* and means "empty and more." Here mind's space cannot be separated from its awareness and bliss. The reformed or "Yellow Hat" school, stays with objective analytical understanding and uses the term *rangtong*, that "everything is empty in its essence," which attracts other kinds of practitioners. Any practices given must be in accordance with Buddha's teachings and gradually prove their worth through an increased quality of life for the student, as well as a growing independence and maturity.

Those who are new to meditation often block themselves needlessly. Whoever wants to accomplish the qualities of the buddhas, however, will have to face three great obstacles, one of which is a lack of confidence. In the beginning, mind's awareness does not yet supply an unshakable basis for all things. One still knows one's ups because of one's downs. As this yo-yo behavior becomes less dramatic due to one's observation of life and increasingly rational style, many do not recognize how well they are already doing and that they are evidently well on their way. The periods of frustration that therefore arise can best be bridged by developing confidence in one's teacher or lineage, by reading their biographies, or simply by continuing with one's practice no matter what. Then flashes of lightness and a generally growing ability to look back will make it clear just how much unnecessary luggage one already discarded. One may also notice mind's timeless bliss-light break through in a moment of expecting nothing—proving everything beyond question. This absence of trust is not the only barrier to overcome, however.

A lack of desire to discriminate harms one's development in a much more lasting way, and in Buddhism this kind of voluntary blindness is unnecessary. Because all beings have buddha nature as their timeless basis, being critical when religions are inhumane or criminal only brings them closer to something positive and benefits their adherents' lives. Whoever will not distinguish between different spiritual paths because they do not want to label anything religious as harmful or "bad" is up in the air and has neither a way nor a goal. It is understandable, though, given the countless instances of religious persecution and war that people with a background in one of the Middle Eastern "contract" religions are burdened with, that they will remain unclear on the definitions. If one thinks that only one truth must fit all and at the same time wants to be peaceful, one must ignore differences between the systems. In the Far East, however, where Buddhism arose, one does not proselytize. One is instead relieved that there exist different spiritual hats for different heads and remains able to distinguish between what fits oneself and what may work for others. Personally, I filter the future visitors to our Diamond Way Centers with provocative statements at my lectures and in my books. They save a great deal of time, both for those who come and for those who therefore stay away.

Whoever is unfamiliar with the texts and claims of different religions or simply cannot fathom the actually quite logical observation that different beings have different expectations and capacities, may also find another solution. They then claim that everything is the same or given by some "god," which clearly are both wrong in Buddhism. Soft, overly-inclusive schools of thought like the New Age movement that are often supposed to contain ultimate wisdom also point to nothing timelessly absolute but stay within the highest conceptual realms. However, they may help beings on the level of practical advice. What is most important is one's trust in space and its perfect and limitless qualities, the view of the Great Seal. Some people however don't even get on to the great freeway towards enlightenment but instead build houses at their very point of entry. They become aura-healers, channelers, knowers of crystals, pyramid experts, interpreters of angels, or teachers about the book produced by some Bhagwhan students called the "Five Tibetans"—a pure fabrication. Of course it is pleasant and maybe meaning-ful to use one's qualities and the best parts of these different spiritual fields for the benefit of others and oneself, but it is truly a pity to lose track of that perfect freeway of under-standable methods and convincing goals because of them. Or to become superstitious or influence the directness of one's development with contents from other systems that are sim-ply something else and don't belong.

The third great hindrance is one's identification with the many abilities and special experiences that appear on one's way. It swallows up masses of "nowness," freshness, and energy. Though such results are of course attractive, holding on to them is comparable to carrying the milestones that one passes and it severely hampers one. The constant evaluation of one's progress and what one can now do becomes an ever more intricate process and destroys the lightness and poten-tial of the here and now. Finally, one ends up with arms like a gorilla and is stuck at the side of the road.

Still, there exists a way that flows, one that brings a steadily growing sense of satisfaction. Whoever has the strength for the difficult stretches, trusting their potential and transmis-sion, whoever dares to take a stand and is willing to see things from a beyond-personal perspective, will increasingly and fluently express mind's pervading strength, love, and the power of space. All qualities will then appear spontaneously, at the right junctures of time and place, and as the sustainable results of a healthy development.

Karmapa here shows how to handle the special qualities produced through one's absorption. Maturing others, training, and perfection are three important activity fields of the bodhisattvas. One here helps beings to develop through any skillful means including the above mentioned miracles that were surely more electrifying seven hundred years ago than today. One works with the purification of their view until they can experience the world as a buddha realm. From that point on, their own development will make them benefit beings in evermore meaningful ways.

Practically, one may compare mind to a house and then look to improve its qualities. In that case, useful behavior would be its foundation, compassion, and wisdom are its space-giving walls, and the view of the Great Seal and the methods of the Diamond Way constitute its potentially vast and ornamental roof. Part of this understanding is also shared by successful mothers or teachers worldwide, to develop the full human potential.

"Train in the Buddhas' pure lands" does not mean planting some nice flowers for all to enjoy. Above all else, it means giving people a chance to change their values and their consciousness. Old age, sickness, death, and loss will not go away while bodies and worlds exist; but anyone can shift their awareness from what is transitory and changing to that which has intrinsic and timeless value. When disturbed personal views fall away, liberating wisdoms and pure realms of experience appear instead. Then all things, inner and outer, radiate in their richness, as expressions of timelessly perfect mind.

To many critical people, the idea of making wishes may seem a bit fishy, but from a Buddhist perspective it contains no dependent or otherwise sticky element. Making wishes means enriching space with meaningful seeds for the benefit of all. In that way, potential appears which will be useful in the long haul. Precisely for this reason, Karmapa chose this format for the statements that he wanted to make. Though one may occasionally abuse one's credit, in the long run one can only obtain what one's accumulation of good impressions makes possible.

The wisest motivation of all is to seek full enlightenment for the good of all beings. Whoever holds this wish will discover that special qualities and intuitive wisdom will arise on their own whenever needed. Under these conditions such spontaneous gifts feel completely right and also function perfectly because they appear from and fit the potential of the moment. After each instance that confirms mind's fearlessness, power, love, and richness, the trick is to happily forget everything and move on with a big heart, open eyes, and little luggage. From a certain level on, all pedantic and egocentric wishes disappear. Conditions change too often, and especially with love it feels strange when the object of our previous deep wishes appears at a time when one is already happily engaged elsewhere. Generally it is wise to leave all details to the Buddhas and simply to wish deeply that all beings reach the highest bliss of enlightenment. As the refuge knows past, present, and future, nothing can here go wrong.

ཚོགས་བཅུའི་རྒྱལ་བ་སྲས་བཅས་ཐུགས་རྗེ་དང་།

May these pure wishes of ourselves and all beings,

རྣམ་དཀར་དགེ་བ་ཇི་སྙེད་ཡོད་པའི་མཐུས།

through the compassion of the buddhas and bodhisattvas of the ten directions

དེ་ལྟར་བདག་དང་སེམས་ཅན་ཐམས་ཅད་ཀྱི།

and the power of all actions that are beneficial and meaningful,

སྨོན་ལམ་རྣམ་དག་ཇི་བཞིན་འགྲུབ་གྱུར་ཅིག།

be fulfilled exactly as they are made.

VERSE 25

With this last verse, all one's enlightened goods have made it past customs and are now packed in a fast car on an autobahn with no speed limit. Countless realizations wait on the clear stretch of road ahead. How then shall we enrich the world?

Using the same words as in his first verse, Karmapa invites his readers to take part in the work. Freshly empowered through the insights he shared and inspired by his eloquent wishes to benefit others, one will surely find the right means.

Seven hundred years ago a motivation through compassion and wisdom was just as fitting as it is today. On its foundation, the view of the Great Seal works like a virus eliminating what is not true. In a beyond-personal way without expectations, it attacks the suffering of beings and destroys its roots.

Thus one's first hopeful inclination that there is a meaning to all things grows into an unshakable certainty. When, from one point to the next, one experiences that the truth and meaning of what is actually there reaches way beyond any imagination or daydream, one is close to the goal. Then one fully uses the potential of the here and now and is conscious in all that happens. Hopefully these wishes for enlightenment by the 3rd Karmapa, now put into a modern Western context, will be the initial spark for the accomplishment of many.

What counts from now on is to nourish the seeds of wisdom planted, to deepen one's view of the Great Seal and to hold it for ever longer periods. Accomplished through short but frequent Diamond Way meditations and not losing one's good feeling in between, one is not merely reviving an outdated Tibetan dream. Today, one's correct view can turn any situation in life into one's teacher; and, with maturity, mind can develop even in the middle of countless distractions. At the beginning of the millennium, in countries around the world with a Western culture, over four hundred Karma Kagyu Diamond Way centers stand ready for lay people and accomplishers to visit. They will be true friends and an excellent guide for one's way. Basis, way, and goal of the Great Seal are here realized on increasingly deep levels by independent people who have critically checked them in their own lives and found them to work. Their basic view is simple: until one has become a Buddha, one should at least try to behave like one.

There is almost certainly a Diamond Way group in or somewhere near your town—greet them from me.

Yours,

Lama Ole

ACKNOWLEDGMENTS

Behind every sucessful man stands an exhausted woman. For the original German edition, it was Caty, but for my English translation I want to thank a man, Doctor Stephen James of our London Center.

It is proven: space is joy.

Appendixes

I. TRADITIONAL OUTLINE

PREPARATION

Verse 1   Paying homage and showing respect.

GENERAL DEDICATION

Verse 2   A general dedication of merit towards enlightenment.

ASPIRATIONS

Verse 3   The general aspiration for support for the path.

Verse 4   The specific aspiration for support for the path.

Verse 5   Aspiration for wisdom to develop on the path.

Verse 6   Aspiration for the faultless path.

Verse 7   What needs to be understood when one practices.

Verse 8   A summary of which practice one needs to do.

Verse 9   Cutting the mistaken view.

Verse 10   All perceived objects are nothing but mind.

Verse 11   The mind has no independent existence in itself.

Verse 12   Abandoning the limitations of being or not being something.

Verse 13   There is no contradiction between emptiness and interdependent expression.

Verse 14   The way discriminating wisdom eliminates mistaken affirmation.

Verse 15   How to reach certainty through meditation and to sustain that state.

Verse 16   Explanation of *shi-ne* or *shamatha*, calm abiding.
Verse 17   Explanation of *lhagthong* or *vipashyana*.
Verse 18   *Lhagtong*, the nature of mind.
Verse 19   *Shi-ne* and *lhagthong* are inseparable.
Verse 20   The meditation experiences that result from
           the practice.
Verse 21   The realization that occurs through the practice.
Verse 22   Identifying compassion.
Verse 23   The inseparability of compassion and emptiness.
Verse 24   Aspiration for the perfect fruit of the path.

CONCLUSION

Verse 25   Dedication of the fulfillment of all positive wishes.

II. OUTLINE

A. PREPARATION

Verse 1

B. MAIN BODY OF THE TEXT, VERSES 2–24

Verse 2   General dedication.

Verses 3–24   Aspirations
Verses 3–4   Aspiration for support for the path.
Verse 5   Aspiration for wisdom developing on the path.
Verse 6   Aspiration for the faultless path.

Verses 7–23   Aspiration of practicing the path correctly.
Verse 7   What should be understood.
Verse 8   A summary of which meditation one
          needs to do.

C. CONCLUSION VERSE 25

III. OUTLINE

A. PREPARATION

Verse 1   Paying homage and showing respect.

B. MAIN BODY OF THE TEXT

Verse 2   General dedication of merit towards enlightenment.

Verse 3   General aspiration for support for the path.

Verse 4   Specific aspiration for support for the path.

Verse 5   Aspiration for wisdom developing on the
path: The wisdom that arises from studying,
from reflection, from meditation.

Verse 6   Aspiration for the faultless path:
Free from the extreme views of eternalism
and nihilism (existence and non-existence).
Free from mistaken affirmation and denial.
Free from the limits of conditioned existence and
inert peace.

Verses 7–23   *Aspiration for practicing the path correctly*

Verse 7   A summary of what one needs to know
when one practices the path, namely:
What is the basis/ground for purification.
What are the means of purification.
What is being purified, and what is the result
of the purification.

The meditation that is to be practiced

Verse 8 A summary of which practice one needs to do:
Cutting doubts away by the view (verses 9–14).
Gaining certitude through meditation (verses 15–23).

Verse 9 Cutting the mistaken view.

Verse 10 All perceived objects are but mind.

Verse 11 The mind has no independent existence in itself.
Abandoning the limitations of the concepts of existing or not existing.

Verse 12 Abandoning the limitations of being or not being something.

Verse 13 There is no contradiction in the emptiness and interdependent expression.

Verse 14 The way discriminating wisdom eliminates mistaken affirmation of what is not there and denial of what appears.

Verse 15 In brief how to reach certainty through meditation and to sustain that state.

Verse 16 *Shi-ne/shamatha/*calm abiding.

Verse 17 Explanation on *lhagthong/vipashyana/*insight.

Verse 18 *Lhagtong*, the nature of mind.

Verse 19 *Shi-ne* and *lhagthong* inseparable.

Verse 20 The meditation experiences that result from the practice: great bliss, clarity and non-conceptuality.

Verse 21 The realization that occurs through the practice.

Verse 22 Identifying compassion.

Verse 23 The inseparability of compassion and emptiness.

Aspiration for the fruition when completing the path

Verse 24 The perfect fruit of the path.

C. CONCLUSION VERSE 25

Verse 25 Dedication of the fulfillment of all positive wishes.

Books by Lama Ole Nydahl

INTRODUCTORY BOOKS
The Way Things Are
A Living Approach to Buddhism for Today's World
O Books Publishing (2008), 240 pages, ISBN: 978-1-84694-042-2

Entering the Diamond Way
Tibetan Buddhism Meets the West
Blue Dolphin Publishing (1985), 251 pages,
ISBN 978-0-931892-03-1

FURTHER READING
Riding the Tiger
The Risks and Joys of Bringing Tibetan Buddhism to the West
Blue Dolphin Publishing (1992), 408 pages,
ISBN 978-0-931892-67-8

The Great Seal: Limitless Space and Joy
The Mahamudra View of Diamond Way Buddhism
Firewheel Publishing (2004), ISBN 978-0-975-2954-0-3

DVD Videos by Lama Ole Nydahl
Secret Journey to East Tibet
A video documentary of a journey made by Lama Ole Nydahl and some
of his friends in 1986 through the forbidden area of east Tibet where they
visited monasteries and other special places as the first Western visitors.

9 1/2 thousand km of Diamond Way
In 1986 Lama Ole Nydahl and his wife Hannah travelled to the then
Soviet Union. There they encountered a great enthusiasm for the
teachings of Tibetan Buddhism. Since then, Lama Ole has toured Russia
every year and established over fifty Diamond Way Buddhist centers and
meditation groups.

LAMA OLE NYDAHL established and currently directs more than six hundred Diamond Way Karma Kagyu Buddhist groups and centers in forty-three countries worldwide. The centers are under the spiritual guidance of the 17th Gyalwa Karmapa, Trinlay Thaye Dorje. The people running the centers and taking part in the centers' activities are lay Buddhist practitioners. They work full-time jobs, while integrating Diamond Way teachings and meditation into their daily lives. Members share responsibility for guiding group meditations, answering questions, and giving explanations about Buddhism. Their work is unpaid, and based on idealism and friendship.

Diamond Way Buddhist Centers Worldwide
http://www.diamondway-buddhism.org

United States
http://www.diamondway.org

Canada
http://www.diamondway-buddhism.ca

United Kingdom
http://www.buddhism.org.uk

Australia
http://www.diamondway.org.au

New Zealand
http://www.diamondway-buddhism.org.nz

Lama Ole Nydahl
http://www.lama-ole-nydahl.org

Other Books by Lama Ole Nydahl
http://www.diamondway.org/publisherspage

Buddhism Today **Magazine**
http://www.buddhism-today.org

A Selection of Buddhist Centers of the Karma Kagyu Lineage
under the spiritual guidance of the 17th Karmapa Trinlay Thaye Dorje
and directed by Lama Ole Nydahl

AUSTRALIA

Buddhist Center Perth
+61 (424) 421123
Perth@diamondway-center.org
www.diamondway.org.au/centres/perth/

Buddhist Center Sydney
+61 (2) 95655331
Sydney@diamondway-center.org
www.diamondway.org.au/centres/sydney/

CANADA

Buddhist Center Calgary
+1 (403) 2558423
Calgary@diamondway-center.org
www.diamondway.org/calgary

Buddhist Center Edmonton
+1 (780) 4555488
Edmonton@diamondway-center.org
www.diamondway.org/edmonton

Buddhist Group Toronto
+1 (416) 8404575
Toronto@diamondway-center.org
www.diamondway.org/toronto

NEW ZEALAND

Buddhist Center Christchurch
+64 (3) 3813108
Christchurch@diamondway-center.org
www.diamondway-buddhism.org.nz

UNITED KINGDOM

Buddhist Center Liverpool
+44 (151) 2223543
Liverpool@diamondway-center.org
www.liverpool.buddhism.org.uk

Buddhist Center London
+44 (20) 79162282
London@diamondway-center.org
www.buddhism-london.org

UNITED STATES OF AMERICA

Buddhist Group Albuquerque
+1 (505) 2563054
Albuquerque@diamondway-center.org
www.diamondway.org/albuquerque

Buddhist Center Austin
+1 (512) 2849081
Austin@diamondway-center.org
www.diamondway.org/austin

Buddhist Center Chicago
+1 (312) 4210133
Chicago@diamondway-center.org
www.diamondway.org/chicago

Buddhist Center Houston
+1 (281) 4366081
Houston@diamondway-center.org
www.diamondway.org/texas/index

Buddhist Center La Crosse
+1 (608) 7841566
Lacrosse@diamondway-center.org
www.diamondway.org/lacrosse

Buddhist Center Los Angeles
+1 (323) 9311903
LosAngeles@diamondway-center.org
www.diamondway.org/la

Buddhist Center Madison
+1 (888) 3915083
Madison@diamondway-center.org
www.diamondway.org/madison

Buddhist Group Maui
+1 (808) 2836849
Maui@diamondway-center.org
www.diamondway.org/maui

Buddhist Center Miami
+1 (305) 7566921
Miami@diamondway-center.org
www.diamondway.org/miami

Buddhist Center Minneapolis
+1 (612) 8255055
Minneapolis@diamondway-center.org
www.diamondway.org/minneapolis

Buddhist Center New York
+1 (212) 2140755
NewYork@diamondway-center.org
www.diamondway.org/ny

Buddhist Group Portland
+1 (503) 4847187
Portland@diamondway-center.org
www.diamondway.org/portland

Buddhist Center San Diego
+1 (858) 4319610
SanDiego@diamondway-center.org
www.diamondway.org/sandiego

Buddhist Center San Francisco
+1 (415) 6616030
SanFrancisco@diamondway-center.org
www.diamondway.org/sf

Buddhist Group Santa Fe
+1 (505) 6035953
SantaFe@diamondway-center.org
www.diamondway.org/santafe/

OTHER COUNTRIES:

AUSTRIA
Buddhist Center Vienna
+43 (1) 2631247
Wien@diamondway-center.org
www.diamantweg.at/wien/

BELGIUM
Buddhist Center Brussels
+32 (2) 5384800
Brussels@diamondway-center.org
www.bouddhisme-voiedudiamant.be

CZECH REPUBLIC
Buddhist Center Prague
+420 (731) 137216
Prague@diamondway-center.org
www.bdc.cz/praha

DENMARK
Buddhist Center København
+45 39292711
Copenhagen@diamondway-center.org
www.buddha-kbh.dk

GERMANY
Buddhist Center Berlin Mitte
+49 (30) 24342544
Berlin-Mitte@diamondway-center.org
www.buddhismus-berlin-mitte.de

Buddhist Center Braunschweig
+49 (531) 798601
Braunschweig@diamondway-center.org
http://www.buddhismus-braunschweig.de/

Buddhist Center Hamburg
+49 (40) 4328380
Hamburg@diamondway-center.org
www.buddhismus-hamburg.de

Buddhist Center Wuppertal
+49 (202) 84089
Wuppertal@diamondway-center.org
http://www.buddhismus-wuppertal.de/

HUNGARY
Buddhist Center Budapest
+36 (1) 3222319
Budapest@diamondway-center.org

IRELAND
Buddhist Center Dublin
+353 (1) 4443014
Dublin@diamondway-center.org

MEXICO
Buddhist Center Mexico City Condesa
+52 (55) 52089190
MexicoCity-Condesa@diamondway-center.org
www.diamondwaymexico.org

POLAND
Buddhist Center Warszawa
+48 (22) 8773408
Warszawa@diamondway-center.org
www.stupahouse.buddyzm.pl

RUSSIA
Buddhist Center St. Petersburg
+7 (812) 3100179
Petersburg@diamondway-center.org
www.petersburg.buddhism.ru

SPAIN
Buddhist Retreat Center Karma Gön
+34 (95) 2115197
KarmaGuen@diamondway-center.org
www.karmaguen.org

SWITZERLAND
Buddhist Center Zürich
+41 (0) 44 3820875
Zurich@diamondway-center.org
www.buddhismus.org/zuerich

VENEZUELA
Buddhist Center Caracas
+58 (212) 2849514
Caracas@diamondway-center.org
www.budismo-camino-del-diamante.org

For a complete and up-to-date list
of Diamond Way Buddhist centers in the above
and many more countries,
as well as more information about
Diamond Way Buddhism,
please visit www.diamondway-buddhism.org.

Made in the USA
Lexington, KY
19 May 2012